The Many Faces
of Information Science

AAAS Selected Symposia Series

Published by Westview Press
1898 Flatiron Court, Boulder, Colorado

for the

American Association for the Advancement of Science
1776 Massachusetts Ave., N.W., Washington, D.C.

The Many Faces of Information Science

Edited by Edward C. Weiss

AAAS Selected Symposium 3

AAAS Selected Symposia Series

Copyright © 1977 by the American Association for the
Advancement of Science

Published in 1977 in the United States of America by

Westview Press, Inc.
1898 Flatiron Court
Boulder, Colorado 80301
Frederick A. Praeger, Publisher and Editorial Director

Library of Congress Cataloging in Publication Data

Main entry under title:

The many faces of information science.

(AAAS selected symposium; 3)
Includes bibliographies.
1. Information science--Congresses. 2. Information
theory--Congresses. 3. Communication--Congresses.
I. Weiss, Edward Craig, 1927-   II. American Association
for the Advancement of Science. III. Series: American
Association for the Advancement of Science. AAAS selected
symposium; 3.

Z699.A1M36   029'.9'5   77-12103
ISBN 0-89158-430-7

Printed and bound in the United States of America

About the Book

The growth in the development of digital technology in the last quarter-century has been phenomenal, yet there is a surprising mismatch between the high capacity of the technology and the logical level at which it is employed for information transfer and retrieval. The problem appears to lie in the state of the discipline itself: we have been trying to develop and apply a technology without a well-developed scientific foundation to support it. A discipline involves three major parts--a science, applications, and education--and each part must support the others. In information science, the weakest component today is the science itself. Two questions emerge: what does information science consist of, and how can we strengthen it to provide a sound theoretical structure from which future applications will derive?

Because the purpose of this volume is to review the current status of information science and to explore possibilities for breakthroughs, the book will be of interest to basic and applied researchers in the fields of information and computer science, to system developers and operators, and to educators and students.

Contents

vii

List of Figures

Foreword

The *AAAS Selected Symposia Series* was begun in 1977 to
provide a means for more permanently recording and more
widely disseminating some of the valuable material which is
discussed at the AAAS Annual National Meetings. The volumes
in this *Series* are based on symposia held at the Meetings
which address topics of current and continuing significance,
both within and among the sciences, and in the areas in which
science and technology impact on public policy. The *Series*
format is designed to provide for rapid dissemination of information, so the papers are not typeset but are reproduced
directly from the camera copy submitted by the authors, without copy editing. The papers are reviewed and edited by
the symposia organizers who then become the editors of the
various volumes. Most papers published in this *Series* are
original contributions which have not been previously published, although in some cases additional papers from other
sources have been added by an editor to provide a more comprehensive view of a particular topic. Symposia may be reports of new research or reviews of established work, particularly work of an interdisciplinary nature, since the AAAS
Annual Meeting typically embraces the full range of the
sciences and their societal implications.

WILLIAM D. CAREY
Executive Officer
American Association for
the Advancement of Science

About the Editor

Edward C. Weiss is program director, Information Science Program, National Science Foundation. He has authored some 30 publications in engineering psychology, systems analysis, and information science.

About the Authors

William Goffman, dean of the School of Library Science at Case Western Reserve University, Cleveland, specializes in communication theory and information systems. He has written numerous papers in these fields.

Marshall C. Yovits is the chairman of the Department of Computer and Information Science at the Ohio State University, Columbus. He is editor of the Advances in Computers *series (Academic Press) and has published many papers on information science. Dr. Yovits specializes in management applications, information science and information systems.*

Lawrence J. Rose, assistant professor of computer and information science at the Ohio State University, Columbus, is co-investigator of an NSF-funded study on information flow and analysis. Dr. Rose's areas of interest are information storage and retrieval and information structures.

Judith G. Abilock, graduate research associate and Ph.D. candidate in the Department of Computer and Information Science at the Ohio State University, Columbus, has authored several papers in the field. Ms. Abilock is specializing in management information systems, decision analysis, man-machine interaction, and accounting.

Naomi Sager is the project director of the Linguistic String Project at New York University. She has been the principal investigator of research projects for NSF and NIH, and has authored numerous publications. Dr. Sager specializes in computational linguistics and computerized natural language processing.

Donald J. Hillman is a professor of information science and director of the Center for Information Science at Lehigh University, Bethlehem, Pennsylvania. He is published widely on classification techniques and mathematical linguistics as it applies to information storage and retrieval.

Vladimir Slamecka, professor and director of the School of Information and Computer Science at the Georgia Institute of Technology, Atlanta, is the author of 4 monographs and 75 papers in this area.

Charls Pearson is a research associate at the School of Information and Computer Science at the Georgia Institute of Technology, Atlanta. He has been responsible for numerous symposia, invited lectures, and papers on information science. He is principle investigator of "Semiotic Foundations of Information Science" and is director of the "Semlab."

Introduction

The papers contained in this volume examine the various faces of information science as an emerging discipline. Each one reflects a different facet of the ferment which is being experienced by this relatively new science. But before the reader explores these research issues and their many subtle interrelationships, it might be of interest to gain an overview of the field from the perspective of a research funding agency.

The basic issue confronting us at this time is that the research and technology base which was established over the past ten to fifteen years is rapidly being depleted by way of applications. We are attempting to meet this challenge by supporting a broad program of research ranging from the very basic to the applied. It is important to continue to provide the means for enhancing existing systems technology, and at the same time establish a theoretical structure which will enable a coherent and systematic approach to future research and development efforts.

The Information Science Program is responsible for supporting the fundamental research knowledge and applied technology base which are essential to accomplishing the major national goals and objectives of the Division of Science Information of the National Science Foundation. It has the primary responsibility for the goal of strengthening information science as an academic discipline in order that applications in science information can begin to be derived in a fashion consistent with the practices of other more established branches of engineering. In the past there were strong expectations, with the emergence of new ideas in cybernetics and information theory and with the development of the digital computer, that we would have a theory of information retrieval from which effective systems would derive. But very little theoretical work on information retrieval has emerged. From a conceptual point of view, we are still at a very primitive level with respect to a theoretical understanding of the full problems of information retrieval.

For instance, technologists attempted to solve the information storage and retrieval problem without first having a measure of the value of information, a theory of information transfer, or an understanding of human information processes. As a result, science information storage and retrieval systems have not met with the huge success originally anticipated. The problem appears to be with the state of the discipline itself. It can be seen that we were trying to develop a technology without having a well-developed scientific foundation upon which to support it.

It is now necessary to provide a theoretical foundation for information transfer which would facilitate the transition of information science from a field to a scientific discipline. Such a transition is necessary for reasons beyond mere academic status. In the absence of an analytical or conceptual framework, a great deal of the activity directed toward the development of information systems and improving techniques of information flow and transfer is taking place on an ad hoc basis. Little, if any, of a common nature exists to provide guidance in systems design and evaluation. If science information systems are to be designed in accordance with usual engineering practices, it will first be necessary to establish a theoretical framework such as exists in chemistry or physics. If a science of information transfer were to emerge, the applications would be in terms of systems developments across a wide range of environments which will include science information systems as well as management information systems, military command and control systems, medical diagnostic systems, educational systems, and general communications systems.

The very concept of information science is, however, the source of frequent definitional controversy. It would be far veyond the scope of this brief introductory paper to attempt to resolve these diverse points of view. But it would seem appropriate, at least, to state the definitional framework of this discussion and the papers which follow.

Information science can be defined as that set of principles and prescriptive rules dealing with the organization, maintenance, and management of bodies of scientific, technical, and business information used in decision-making. Information transfer then can be viewed as a communication problem. It is concerned with improving the communication of recorded information among three types of individuals or groups: (1) the originator of information; (2) the processor of information; (3) the user of information. Thus, information science must be an organized body of knowledge based on explanatory principles which seeks to discover and formulate in general terms the conditions under which facts and events relating to the generation, transmission, and use of information occur. This would suggest three levels of problems for investigation at the highest level of definition,

namely the technical, semantic, and effectiveness problems. Phenomena basic to these problems are signal transmission such as Shannon's work in information theory in the
technical problem area, meaning in the semantic problem area,
and relevance in the effectiveness problem area. Signal
transmission is the province of electrical engineering and to
a lesser extent computer science. Information science is
concerned with the problems of meaning and relevance, but
only as they apply to the generation, transmission and use
of organized bodies of information which distinguishes it
from the more fundamental domain of linguistics.

Within the boundaries of this rather broad definition
we are supporting a wide range of research projects from the
very theoretical to the applied. But the papers presented
in this volume are focused at the basic end of the spectrum.
The rationale for the support of this type of research de-
rives from a Roundtable on Research in Information Science,
which was chaired by Dr. Vladimir Slamecka, who is Director
of the School of Information and Computer Science at the
Georgia Institute of Technology. This conference, which was
supported by the National Science Foundation, was held in May
of 1975 at Anaheim, California[1]. This report states that
with very few exceptions the scientist is not the sole or
final authority over the selection of problems he decides to
study. Societal forces and pressures which influence the
course and subject of research must be considered. From this
standpoint, it is recognized that the framework for future
information science research is given by the imminent preoccupation of society with the prudent and cost-effective
management of knowledge as a social resource. This societal
objective considerably extends and modifies the framework of
past research in information science.

In the past, when speaking of "information resources" we
have usually meant collections and repositories of physical
records or information-containing packages. In the context
of our new framework, the resource is knowledge or the cumu-
lative content of these repositories, regardless of their
physical packaging. Information management refers to efficient bibliographic organization and inventory control.
Knowledge management refers to the principles, policies, and
practices for guiding and controlling, in a socially and
technically optimal sense, the generation, distribution, consumption and effect of this resource. One major, visible
result of this change will be new generations of information
systems which will permit interaction between man and stored

[1]V. Slamecka, Long-Range Research Objectives in Information
Science, Final Report to the Division of Science Information
of the National Science Foundation; School of Information and
Computer Science, Georgia Institute of Technology, Oct. 1975.

knowledge, rather than between man and stored document descriptions. Finally, it must be recognized that these systems
will operate in a networking environment.

It should be unnecessary to argue on behalf of fundamental research in pursuit of such objectives. We are, after
all, in the business of expanding options not procuring the
future by bits and pieces. Without theory, the work of practitioners will constantly be questioned and doubted. It
should also be unnecessary to debate meanings of distinctions
among the notions of fundamental science, pure science, basic
science, theoretical science, applied science, etc. We must
investigate phenomena as and where they occur in nature, as
well as practice-oriented processes which are frequently
identified as systems research. But the papers presented
in this volume, as was stated previously, deal only with
the more basic end of the spectrum.

The first paper by Goffman was motivated by the fact
that information science lacks the theoretical foundations of
well-established scientific disciplines. The objective of
the study was to develop a general theory of information
transfer by synthesizing the epidemic, genetic, and dif-
fusion models which were adapted from the disciplines of
epidemiology, biology, and physics. The resulting synthesis
of these models is expected to aid in formulating a theoretical basis for information science as a scientific discipline.

The second paper, by Yovits, deals with the development
of a general theory of information flow which is designed to
permit the analysis and quantification of information. The
theory is primarily concerned with information uses in decision-making environments. Thus, it can be considered as a
pragmatic theory of information which, beyond its theoretical
and conceptual interest, should have major and immediate
applications for the development of information systems and
networks, as well as for the general understanding of information flow, retrieval, and transfer.

The next two papers are somewhat related in that they
are both aimed at establishing the basis for knowledge or fact
delivery systems. The work of Sager at New York University
is investigating the repeated information structures of
science language by sub-discipline. The results indicate
that scientific writing contains repeated structures which
house the textual information in repeated ways. These structures can be looked upon as the counterpart in language materials to tables in the case of numerical data. They contain
the factual material of the science, and they differ in
appropriate ways for different sciences. The results will
find eventual applications in complex information processing,
such as the combining of information sources in large knowledge transfer systems and the interpreting of user's natural
language queries at the input to such systems.

The work of Hillman at Lehigh University is an exploration and evaluation of the underlying technology for the retrieval of factual information. It has produced a model of a knowledge transfer system which will enable a scientific user to obtain specific answers concerning an area of research. For example, he could obtain descriptions of the hypotheses which were tested, the instrumentation which was used, or the quantitative data which were analyzed, as well as the results of the analyses depending upon his search question. And it would do this for all relevant articles contained in the information bank which was being queried. It has also produced the very rudimentary statements of a theory of information regeneration which when combined with the work of Sager at New York University, will eventually provide the basis for natural language systems capable of retrieving factual relationships and even inferences from the articles assembled in a data base, rather than merely the citation to the documents as is the case with present systems.

The final paper by Pearson and Slamecka is based on the underlying thesis that semiotics, the science of signs and sign processes, is the major element of the scientific foundations of information technology and that in studies of information measures, in human processing of information, in linguistic investigations of natural language, and in artificial communication systems, the essential question is "What is a sign, and what kind of structure does it have?" The object of the study is to determine the structure of various types of signs, and the relationship between sign structure and information properties. The results of this research will contribute not only to the development of the foundations of information science, but also to its practical applications in as diverse areas as information transfer, compiler and retrieval languages, and the effectiveness of communication processes.

I would like to extend my sincere thanks to our distinguished researchers for providing us with this glimpse of a few of the many faces of information science.

On the Dynamics of Communication

William Goffman

Information Science, regardless of how it may be defined, must be concerned with the phenomenon of communication, namely the process by which information is conveyed among the members of a population, be they living organisms, devices or some combination of these. Weaver has suggested three broad levels of communication problems. (1) These are:

1. The Technical or Engineering problem dealing with the accuracy with which the symbols of communication are transmitted.

2. The Semantic or Language problem dealing with the precision with which the transmitted symbols convey the desired information.

3. The Effectiveness or Relevance problem dealing with the effectiveness with which the received information affects conduct in the desired way.

Level 1 basically deals with signal transmission and noise, but level 2 must deal primarily with the ambiguous notion of meaning whereas level 3 must deal with the equally ambiguous notion of relevance, since the precision with which the transmitted symbols convey the desired information depends on their meaning to both sender and receiver and the effectiveness with which the received information affects behavior depends on its relevance to the receiver.

Although the three levels of communication are not independent, the technical and semantic levels are clearly mechanisms for conveying relevant information among the members of the population.

Overall the most formidable problems in communication relate to 1) what is meant by information and how we shall agree to measure it; 2) what is meant by relevance and how we shall agree to measure it; 3) what is meant by meaning and how we shall agree to measure it. In the classical Shannon Theory (2) information is treated as the removal of uncertainty. Formally, Shannon's view of information is associated with the notion of a finite scheme, i.e., a set of mutually exclusive and exhaustive events each of whose probability of occurrence p_i is known. The uncertainty of the scheme is measured by the function

$$H = - \sum_i p_i \log p_i$$

which is a measure of the amount of information obtained once the uncertainty is removed. Shannon proved that the form of the function H called the entropy of the scheme is unique given the following desireable properties:

1. H is defined for a set of non-negative real numbers whose sum is 1.

2. H is maximum when all of these numbers are equal to each other.

3. H is additive.

4. The introduction of the impossible event does not alter the value of H.

Thus, in Shannon's view information depends upon choice, and, the greater the number of equally likely choices, the greater the amount of information once the choice is made. Moreover, given the properties which one would expect of such a measure, it must be of a certain form, namely $-\lambda \sum_i p_i \log p_i$ where λ is a constant.

The Shannon Theory, though very elegant, claims only to address the technical level of communication independent of the other two. In this report I shall attempt to address communication from the point of view of the effectiveness level independent of the other two. I shall thus give primary concern to the notion of relevance. Moreover, since communication is a time dependent phenomenon, I shall concentrate on establishing certain general dynamic properties of the process.

Consider an arbitrary population N whose members are conveying information among each other at time t. Every element x in N is thus transmitting a set of symbols $\{\bar{x}\}$ at time t. Hence, associated with the population N is a set $\bar{N}$ representing the symbols of communication transmitted by the members of N at time t.

Since two or more members of N may be transmitting identical symbols, it follows that 1) the mappings of N onto $\bar{N}$ and conversely are not necessarily one to one, and 2) there may exist an informational overlap among the members of N. For a given population N we can define a measure of informational overlap R_{ij} of an element x_j relative to an element x_i. Such a measure can take on a variety of forms but would be expected to possess the following properties:

1. R_{ij} is minimal when the informational overlap between x_i and x_j is 0, i.e., x_i and x_j transmit no common symbols.

2. R_{ij} is maximal when x_i and x_j always transmit identical symbols.

3. R_{ij} is not equal to R_{ji} except for the maximal and minimal values since the informational overlap of x_j relative to x_i need not be the same as the informational overlap of x_i relative to x_j.

4. For convenience R takes on values from 0 to 1.

The simplest measure possessing the above properties is the ratio of common symbols transmitted to the total number transmitted at a point in time. Thus $R_{ij}(t) = m(x_i \wedge x_j)/m(x_i)$ where $m(x_i \wedge x_j)$ is the number of common symbols transmitted by x_i and x_j at time t and $m(x_i)$ the number of symbols transmitted by x_i.

The time t should be thought of as a small time interval Δt rather than an instantaneous point in time since the symbols of communication are transmitted in sequence rather than simultaneously. The measure R_{ij} might be thought of as the conditional probability that x_j will transmit a symbol of communication $\bar{x}$ in the time interval Δt given that x_i has transmitted $\bar{x}$ in the same time interval.

By a similar argument we can define a measure of overlap R_{kl} between symbols $\bar{x}_k$ and $\bar{x}_l$. For convenience, however, we shall develop our subsequent arguments only in terms of N, although they could be similarly developed for $\bar{N}$.

Since communication is a time dependent phenomenon, the measure of informational overlap between two elements x_i and x_j may vary in time. That is, the informational states of elements in N may undergo change. This change essentially takes place when an element x_j receives symbols of communication from an element x_i which it absorbs and assimilates with its own store of symbols. This in turn puts x_j in a position to both receive and transmit new symbols of communication.

We say that if $R_{ij}(t)$ is greater than some number τ, $0 \leq \tau \leq 1$, then x_i converses with x_j relative to τ. τ can be thought of as a threshold establishing the level of effective informational overlap of x_j relative to x_i at time t. We then prove that a necessary condition for $R_{ij}^i(t+\triangle t) > \tau$ i.e., for x_i to converse with x_j relative to τ at time $t+\triangle t$, is that there exist a sequence of elements in N from x_i to x_j such that $R_{j-1,j}(t) > \tau$. That is, that there exist a sequence of elements connecting x_i with x_j such that adjacent elements converse at time t. We call such a sequence a communication chain and say that two elements connected by such a chain communicate. If there also exists a communication chain from x_j to x_i, we say that x_i and x_j intercommunicate relative to τ at time t. Thus, a necessary condition for an element x_i in N to converse with x_j in N at time $t+\triangle t$, is that x_i communicate with x_j at time t; and for them to converse with each other at time $t+\triangle t$, that they intercommunicate at time t. This means that if x_i does not converse with x_j at time t, their informational states are altered in the time interval $\triangle t$ to where the informational overlap of x_j relative to x_i now exceeds the threshold τ. This is equivalent to saying that at time t, x_i converses with x_j at a lower threshold, which implies that as t increases τ tends to decrease. We can thus think of the threshold as a decreasing function of time.

It is interesting to note that the relationship of conversance is reflexive but neither symmetric nor transitive; that the relation of communication is reflexive and transitive but not symmetric; and that the relation of intercommunication is reflexive, symmetric and transitive. Thus, for a given value of τ, hence at any point in time the relation of communication defines a pre-order and the relation of intercommunication an equivalence relation on the population N. Consequently, at any given point in time, the population N can be partitioned into intercommunication classes which cover the entire population. Furthermore, there may exist elements belonging to distinct classes which

communicate, albeit they don't intercommunicate. Therefore,
the population N at any point in time can be represented by
disjoint sets of communicating intercommunication classes.
It can be shown easily that the shortest intercommunication
chain between two elements at a given point in time, i.e.,
at a given threshold, constitutes a distance between those
elements at that point in time and that the shortest communication chain between two elements constitutes a quasi-
distance between the two elements. If two elements do not
communicate, than the distance between them is said to be
infinite. Consequently, the population N possesses a well
defined structure, namely it can be classified, ordered and
is metrizable.

If x_i converses with x_j at time t, we say that x_i is
relevant to x_j. This implies that x_i communicates with x_j
at time $t - \triangle t$. Thus, x_i is relevant to x_j only if x_i
communicates with x_j. We justify the above definition of
relevance as follows. The notion of relevance has for many
years been of interest to logicians as well as information
scientists. In this respect, I quote from the writings of
A.R. Anderson and N.D. Belnap. (3)

"For more than two millenia logicians have taught that
a necessary condition for the validity of an inference
from A to B is that A be relevant to B. Virtually every
logic book up to the present century has a chapter on
fallacies of relevance, and many contemporary elementary
texts have followed the same plan. (Notice that contemporary writers, in the later and more formal chapters
of their books, seem explicitly to contradict the
earlier chapters, when they try desperately to con the
students into accepting material or strict "implication" as a "kind" of implication relation, in spite of
the fact these relations countenance fallacies of relevance.) But the denial that relevance is essential to
a valid argument (a denial which is implicit in the
view that strict "implication" is an implication relation) seems to us flatly in error.

"Imagine, if you can, a situation as follows. A mathematician writes a paper on Banach spaces, and after
proving a couple of theorems he concludes with a conjecture. As a footnote to the conjecture, he writes:
"In addition to its intrinsic interest, the conjecture
has connections with other parts of mathematics which
might not immediately occur to the reader. For example,
if the conjecture is true, then the first order functional calculus is complete; whereas if it is false,
then it implies that Fermat's last conjecture is correct.

"The editor replies that the paper is obviously acceptable but he finds the final footnote perplexing; he can
see no connection whatever between the conjecture and
the "other parts of mathematics", and none is indicated
in the footnote. So the mathematician replies, "Well,
I was using 'if...then -' and 'implies' in the way that
logicians have claimed I was: the first order functional calculus is complete, and necessarily so, so
anything implies that fact - and if the conjecture is
false it is presumably impossible, and hence implies
anything. And if you object to this usage, it is simply
because you have not understood the technical sense of
'if...then -' worked out so nicely for us by logicians."
And to this the editor counters: "I understand the
technical bit all right, but it is simply not correct.
In spite of what most logicians say about us, the standards maintained by this journal require that the antecedent of an 'if...then -' statement must be relevant
to the conclusion drawn. And you have given no evidence
that your conjecture about Banach spaces is relevant
either to the completeness theorem or to Fermat's
conjecture."

"The editor's point is of course that though the technical meaning is clear, it is simply not the same as
the meaning ascribed to "if...then -" in the pages of
his journal (nor, we suspect, in the pages of this
JOURNAL). Furthermore, he has put his finger precisely on the difficulty: to argue from the necessary
truth of A to if B then A is simply to commit a fallacy
of relevance. The fancy that relevance is irrelevant to
validity strikes us as ludicrous, and we therefore make
an attempt to explicate the notion of relevance of A
to B."

Belnap and Anderson go on to show that the proof of an ade-
quate deduction theorem where relevance is demanded would
require the validity of a certain set of inferences. "It
then seems plausible," they say, "to consider the following
axiomatic system as capturing the notion of relevance."
These are the axioms of identity, transitivity, permutation
and self distribution. It is easy to show that the relation
of communication as defined above satisfies these axioms.
Hence, the notion of relevance as defined above would seem
to be consistent with the notion of relevance as defined by
Anderson and Belnap in logic. As a consequence, the population N possesses a structure defined on the basis of relevance. Each communication chain represents a string of elements connected on the basis of relevance and each intercommunication class represents a network of elements such

that every pair is of finite distance from each other. The distance or quasi-distance between elements represents the minimal number of steps required for relevant information to flow from one member of N to another. Clearly, for every value of τ , hence at every point in time, N can be represented as a relevance graph with each intercommunication class being a connected subgraph. Moreover, the condensation graphs represent the communication relation between inter-communication classes. Every connected subgraph of a condensation graph is a partially ordered set of intercommunication classes, the order relation being that of communication, hence relevance.

As τ ranges from 1 to 0, i.e., as t goes from 0 to infinity, the associated family of relevance graphs describes the dynamics of communication among the members of N. That is, the structure of N tends to go from a set of unit elements at τ = 1 to a single intercommunication class of diameter 1 at τ = 0. Thus, the population N undergoes a sequence of contraction mappings onto itself. In other words, the diverse elements of N tend to be synthesized into fewer elements of greater complexity. When such a process is carried out, information is obtained and the diversity of the population is eliminated. Thus, information consists in removing diversity which existed before the synthesis took place. The larger this diversity, the larger the amount of information obtained by removing it.

The next question is how to measure the diversity. It would seem to be desirable for such a measure to possess the following properties:

1. It is minimum when all elements are connected.

2. It is maximum when all elements are disconnected.

3. It has the additive property.

4. Introduction into the population N of an element conveying no symbols of communication does not alter the measure.

But clearly these are the same properties required of Shannon's entropy measure. Hence, if we can find numbers greater or equal to 0 which sum to one and represent the overall diversity of the population, the uniqueness theorem tells us that the diversity measure must be of the same form as the entropy measure. Consider an arbitrary threshold τ . On the basis of τ , N is partitioned into a set of intercommunication classes. Let N_i be the number of elements in the ith class. Then N_i/N over all i are a set of non-negative real numbers which sum to one and which represent the diversity of N at threshold τ or at the given point in time represented by τ . Consequently,

$$D_\tau = - \sum_i N_i/N \log N_i/N$$

can serve as a suitable measure of the diversity of the population N. Clearly, the measure D possesses the required properties. It is maximum when all the N_i/N are equal which represents the most diverse state of N since all classes contain the same number of elements, and it is minimal when N is totally connected. If we now let τ vary from 1 to 0, we get

$$D = \sum_\tau D_\tau$$

which constitutes a measure of the amount of information obtained by the process of synthesizing diverse sets of elements over the interval represented by the range of the threshold τ . The synthesizing effect of each element x in N on the other members can be established by removing x from N and computing the resulting diversity measure for all values of τ . If the removal of x leads to greater diversity in N then x is a synthesizer. It is thus possible to compare the synthesizing effect of each member of N.

Let us now consider the gross dynamics of communication in the population N as its members go through the synthesizing process. Let X denote the number of connected elements and let Y denote the number of disconnected elements of N at threshold τ . Now let ξ be the change in X in the interval $\Delta \tau$.

Then $\Delta X/\Delta \tau = \xi XY/XY = \sim XY : \alpha = \xi/XY$.

However, since τ is a function of time we have

$\Delta X/\Delta t = \beta XY$. Letting Δt go to 0 yields $dX/dt = \beta XY$ which describes the gross dynamics of communication in the population N. If we assume that β is constant this equation is identical to the Kermack-McKendrick equation for describing a simple epidemic process in a constant population where β is the rate of infection, Y the number of susceptibles and X the number of infectives, both being functions of time. The equation for describing the gross dynamics of communication can easily be generalized to take into account elements leaving N as well as an influx of new members. The general process would be described by the following system of differential equations:

$$dY/dt = -\beta XY + \mu$$

$$dX/dt = \beta XY - \gamma X$$

where γ is the rate of removal of elements from N and μ
the rate of influx of new elements into N. In general, this
system of equations cannot be solved. However, in the special case where X + Y is constant, that is, where the population is in a state of equilibrium in terms of influx and
removal of members, an exact solution can be obtained. In
fact, in this case the system of equation is reduced to an
equation identical in form to the differential equation
describing a population growth process under the constraint
of limited resources (4) which is of course the case where
N is in a state of equilibrium.

Solution of the above equations provides us with a means
of describing and predicting the behavior of the communication process within a population. In particular we can
establish the conditions under which the population of
synthesized elements will increase and the point in time at
which this process will reach a peak.

I shall now briefly discuss two possible areas of application. These relate to information retrieval and to establishment of a funding policy by a granting agency. Let us
first translate the abstract notions discussed above into
concrete terms. The distinguished British physicist Prof.
John Ziman has stated that in his opinion the system of
scientific communication via the published literature
developed over the past 300 years may indeed be the primary
reason for western preeminence in science. (5) Although
from that time on this system has been subject to attack and
discontent, even today it remains the most important and
most effective means of scientific communication.

In terms of the scientific literature, let N be a set
of authors. Then the symbols of communication among the
population of authors N would be the set of Papers $\overline{N}$ produced by the members of N. Clearly both N and $\overline{N}$ vary with
time. Let us first consider a very simple interpretation of
the preceeding abstract notions. We say that two elements of
N converse at time t if they co-author a paper at time t.
Consequently, at any point in time the set of authors N can
be represented by a set of disjoint intercommunication
classes of co-authors with the property that between any two
authors of a given class there exists a chain of co-author-
ships leading from one to the other. In this particular case
the distance between authors is metric rather than quasi-
metric. At any point in time we can compute the diversity

measure D in the population N and identify the key synthe-
sizers among the members of N.   Furthermore, we can describe
the gross dynamics of the population N in terms of the rate
of change of active contributors in N by means of the general epidemic equations.   Consequently, we can identify those
classes of authors which are in an epidemic state, i.e.,
where the rate of change of active contributors is increasing and those classes of authors where the rate of change of
contributors is either decreasing or stable.   One could
assume that those areas of activity represented by classes
of authors in an epidemic state in turn represent areas of
increasing interest to the scientific community whereas the
others are areas whose interest is either past or not yet
developed.   One could then establish the structure defined
above for the symbols of communication of classes of authors
in epidemic states, namely the papers,which provides an
organized file for retrieval purposes.   For example, relevant papers will be connected to each other at various
thresholds.   One could then retrieve relevant documents from
a known relevant document, which is the most common retrieval situation, by identifying all documents within a certain
distance from the imput document at the appropriate threshold.   One could also identify the high synthesizer authors
and papers which could act as points of imput if relevant
documents are not initially known.   On the other hand,
konwledge of the areas of major interest and key synthe-
sizers within these areas could be valuable indicators in
setting science funding policy.   This is not to say that
only the increasingly active areas and their key synthe-
sizers should be supported, but it is clear that these
individuals and groups and areas of interest should be
funded.   Finally, the applications suggested above as well
as others could be carried out using more sophisticated
measures of information overlap thanwere suggested.   For
example, the set N could be collections of journals and the
symbols of communication the papers published by these
journals.   The fact that associated with these papers are
both sets of journals and authors leads to the interesting
study of communication as an epidemic process with inter-
mediate host where the authors represent the definitive
host and the journals the intermediary host. (6) On the
other hand, the papers themselves could be considered to be
the set N and the symbols of communication $\overline{N}$ could be index
terms, references, citations or combinations of these and
other bibliographic devices.   In any event, the procedure
for carrying out this type of analysis is not difficult and
in fact can be automated easily.   There is considerable
experimental evidence supporting many of the assertions
made above, some of which has already been reported in the

literature. (7) The formal details of the work presented here both theoretical and experimental shall be fully reported in the near future.

References

1. Shannon, C.E. and Weaver, W. The Mathematical Theory of Communication, The University of Illinois Press, Urbana, 1963.

2. Khinchin, A.I. Mathematical Foundations of Information Theory, Dover Publications, N.Y., 1957.

3. Anderson, A.R. and Belnap, N.P. "The Pure Calculus of Entailment," Journal of Symbolic Logic, Vol. 27, No. 1 (March 1962).

4. Shaw, W.M. "A Mathematical Analysis of the Growth of a Subject Literature." (to appear)

5. Ziman, S. "Information, Communication and Knowledge," Nature, Vol. 224 (October 25, 1969).

6. Goffman, W. and Warren, K.S. "The Ecology of Medical Literatures," American Journal of Medical Science, Vol. 263, No. 4 (1972).

7. Goffman, W. "A Mathematical Method for Analyzing the Growth of a Scientific Discipline," Journal of ACM, Vol. 18, No. 2 (April 1971).

2

Development of a Theory of Information Flow and Analysis

Marshall C. Yovits, Lawrence Rose, and Judith Abilock

Abstract

This paper describes research being carried out at The Ohio State University leading toward a general theory of information flow and analysis. The objectives of the National Science Foundation-sponsored research program[†] include the following: (1) to develop a theory of information flow and analysis; (2) to identify important parameters and variables in the information process which can be quantified and measured; (3) to develop relationships among the variables which describe their behavior and limitations; (4) to apply this theory to specific practical situations, particularly those involving science information; and (5) to develop both simulation and experimental models for quantification and validation of the theory.

The generalized model of information flow is shown to represent virtually any decision situation. Using this model we derive a number of measures. Two of the more important ones are: $I = m \sum_{i=1}^{m} P(a_i)^2 - 1$ and

$$DME = \left[\sum_{i=1}^{m} P(a_i) \; EV^*_i \right] / max \; (EV^*_k).$$ With these measures we can quantify the amount of information (I) in a decision state and evaluate decision-maker effectiveness (DME). We can also determine the value of information through its

---

† This material is based upon research supported by the National Science Foundation, Division of Science Information, under Grant Numbers GN 41628 and DSI 76-21949.

effect on *DME*. Rules are derived for use by the decision-maker for assimilating new data in his estimates of values and for use in determining selection probabilities for various courses of action. These rules enable feedback, learning, and alternative selection to be modeled, measured, and evaluated. Research is underway to validate the model realistically and to apply it to practical situations.

A further possible result of this research is the development of a decision calculus which will establish guidelines for decision-making given certain situations. These guidelines should permit quantification of the importance of information in the decision-making process.

Background

In several previous papers *(1,2,3)*, we have discussed some of the properties which should exist if information science is ever to become a "true" science similar to physics or chemistry. It has been pointed out that a number of analytical expressions and concepts should exist which can be used to describe and analyze information flow. A framework, called a "generalized information system" was suggested which permits the development of these concepts and expressions.

The word "information" takes on a variety of meanings depending upon the context in which it is used. Our approach relates information to its effectiveness and thus its use and value. Information is frequently used rather specifically in the sense of the Shannon and Weaver "information theory" (more accurately called "communication theory"). In this sense the context of the message is of no significance; the theory is concerned with the probability of the receipt of any particular message for various conditions of the transmission system. While this may be of interest in information science, it is certainly not the major nor even a large part of information science. Such a treatment does not consider the vital areas of concern, almost all of which are involved with the context, meaning, and effectiveness of the message. For these reasons, the Shannon and Weaver approach is generally regarded as too restrictive to be a basis for the formulation of an information science. At the other extreme, the treatment of information to be synonymous with knowledge appears to be far too broad to lead to meaningful and useful principles or relationships in information science.

In our formulation we treat information to be *data of value in decision-making*. Later in the paper we define information quantitatively and rigorously. While our formulation may somewhat delimit the total range of interest in an

intellectual sense, it *does* have virtually universal applica-
bility with regard to any potential applications for information. The authors also feel that any more general definition
is not amenable to the quantification and conceptualization
necessary to establish meaningful relationships. An implication of this definition then is that information is used *only*
for decision-making and that the decision maker has *only* the
resource of information available to him. Thus, information
and decision-making are very closely bound together in our
general model.

Levels of Information

Research in the general area of information theory
started in the mid-1940's. The basic theory, as already
noted, was established with the fundamental work of Claude
Shannon and Warren Weaver *(4,5)*. This theory covers the
transmission of messages over a channel, independent of meaning. Their defined measure of information, which relates to
the entropy of the interpretation of the sequence of bits
transmitted, bears little relation to the layman's concept of
information. This is acknowledged by Weaver, who defines
three levels of information, the first of which (the technical level) is his concern.

The second level of information is concerned with the
meaning of information - its semantic content. Significant
research in this area has been performed by Carnap, Bar-
Hillel, Winograd, and others *(6,7)*. Their research has
attempted to measure the semantic content of simple declarative sentences within their language system. In this context, they do not refer explicitly to the process of communication between individuals. While the level 1 information
definition is concerned with the successful transmission of a
message from point a to point b, the level 2 definition of
information is concerned with the successful interpretation
or understanding of a message once it is received.

The third level of information deals with the effectiveness of information - i.e., how information, once received
and understood, is utilized. Hence the level 3 model is
imbedded in a decision-making environment, since that is the
only framework in which one can observe information utilization. Little research has thus far been accomplished in this
area, even though it is probably the area of greatest significance, interest, and application *(8,9,10,11)*. Our research
is in this area in an effort to develop a general and useful
theory of information *(1,2,3)*.

Effectiveness of Information

Research by several authors has been previously performed in an effort to define an effectiveness or pragmatic
information measure. MacKay *(12)* defines the value of any
data item to be the base 10 logarithm of the ratio of the
performance of the system after and before receipt of the
data. Just how one defines "system performance" is left open
by MacKay.

Cherry *(13)* argues that information aids the decision-
maker by narrowing the range of hypotheses. Information thus
reduces decision-maker uncertainty by narrowing his range of
viable alternatives. The information measure Cherry introduces is the logarithm of the ratio of the aposteriori and
apriori probabilities of selecting an alternative and is
based upon Bayes theorem.

Goffman *(14)* also considers a measure for effectiveness
of information which satisfies all of the desirable properties of the Shannon measure. This measure quantifies the
amount of non-redundant information in a system comprised of
many communicators. Goffman's information measure is much
like the Shannon entropy measure, but relates more to defining "connectedness" via information flow between the elements
of the system.

Our research considers information in the domain of
decision-making and a conceptual decision-maker (DM). It is
important to consider information in a decision-making
environment inasmuch as it is necessary to measure the effect
of the information on the recipient (decision-maker). This
can be done only by monitoring the DM's actions and the
observables resulting from the decisions made. We have
chosen to focus upon all data incoming to the DM in an effort
to quantify the informative content of that data. Our information measure thus relates input data to its effect upon the
decision-making process as shown below.

It is apparent that information - if considered from the
effectiveness point of view - is heavily concerned with the
decision process, and therefore it is important to consider
information and decision making together. While the fundamental objectives of the current research are to develop a
theoretical formulation for a basic theory of information
flow and analysis, we believe that this cannot be done without considering in detail the use of the information; that
is, for making decisions.

There is, of course, a great body of literature in the decision-making field. Some of the typical references are by such researchers as Morris *(15)*, Raiffa *(16)*, Schlaiffer *(17)*, and Radnor *(18)*. An excellent survey by Bandyopadhyay *(19)* provides further references to research in this area. Unfortunately, we find that the approaches described in the literature are neither general enough nor sufficiently flexible to represent the situation adequately with regard to the use of information. In particular, there is little in the literature pertaining to the non-expert decision maker, whereas information will be of perhaps greatest value in this situation. Furthermore, we believe it is necessary to consider the *entire* decision process which is generally repetitive over periods of time. This process heavily involves feedback information using the results of previous decisions.

The General Model

Our general model of information flow and analysis is illustrated in Figure 1, and we briefly describe its operation. This model can be used to describe most, if not all, information-dependent activities. It provides a way of looking at any information-decision interaction and defining the role and flow of information in the system. The IAD module (Information Acquisition and Dissemination) processes data for the system. Both exogenous (external environmental) and endogenous (internal feedback) data are acquired by the IAD module. Whenever a decision must be made, the DM module (using all of the data available) establishes the possible courses of action and selects the "best" one to execute. The Execution module executes the DM-chosen course of action, according to all pertinent external environmental factors, leading to various outcomes depending on the alternative executed. These outcomes will be some *observable* quantities. They must be observable in a physical sense if they are to have any effect. The Transformation module takes all observables of the alternative executed and turns these observations into data. These data are fed back into the IAD module and we have come full circle, following the flow of information in the model.

This model of a generalized information system rests upon three basic hypotheses:

H1. Information is data of value in decision-making;
H2. Information gives rise to observable effects;
H3. Information feedback exists so that the Decision Maker will adjust his model for later similar decisions.

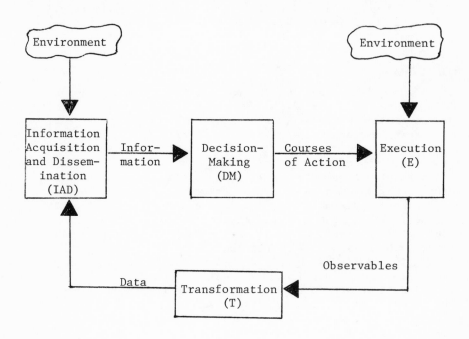

Figure 1:   The Generalized Information System Model

The first hypothesis requires that information be used in a decision-making context. If information is received, but never used or applied to a subsequent decision, then its effect does not exist and it cannot be measured. Hypothesis 2 assures that if the decision-maker (DM) does make a decision, then the outcome of that decision can be observed and measured. This precludes decision-making in a vacuum. Observables must exist if the decision-making and the courses of action are to be evaluated. Hypothesis 3 indicates that the DM learns from feedback data resulting from previous decisions. Note that the observed outcomes of repetitive or related decision-making situations provide data upon which future decisions will be made.

Generalized Decision Making

This model is dynamic in nature: even in a stationary decision situation the DM's model may well change with time. A DM learns about his particular decision situation and environment as follows:

1. He makes a decision (chooses a course of action) on the basis of all information available to him;
2. He predicts some probable outcomes;
3. He compares actual resulting observables against his predicted observables (feedback learning);
4. He updates his total model of the situation as a result of this process;
5. He returns to step 1.

For any problem environment, a DM attempts to fulfill two main objectives:

1. To choose the "best" course of action (c.o.a.) according to some criterion given his state of knowledge;
2. To learn the most about the total existing situation from the decision-making process.

It is important to note that a DM has these two main objectives in choosing a course of action. "Classical" decision theory says that a DM always chooses that c.o.a. that maximizes some criteria. This is a considerable oversimplification, and the DM in fact does not automatically choose the c.o.a. with highest expected return. This is true for at least three reasons. First, because the DM may be unsure of his estimates; second, he may wish to learn more about the total situation by executing alternatives other than the one with highest expected return; and third, the situation may be changing with time, or if not the DM must generally assure himself that it is a static situation.

Learning from any c.o.a. executed is in fact a very important objective of decision-making. The DM does this by
monitoring the outcomes resulting from the decision. This
feedback updates the DM's data base upon which decisions are
based. Given the outcome of earlier decisions, then how will
the DM update his data base? If the outcome data matches the
DM's expectations, then his confidence will rise even though
there may be no other change in his estimates. However, if
the expected and actual results vary, then the DM will incor-
porate these new data into his current estimates. He learns
from the deviation between his expected values of the outcomes and the actual values. Learning is similar to sampling
from a distribution and predicting the underlying theoretical
distribution. The better the DM's learning capability, the
better his expected performance. The action of learning updates the DM's state of knowledge, with input arriving as
either external or feedback data as illustrated in Figure 1.
Learning increases the DM's confidence in his perception of
the decision situation. Learning more about a given situation further removes uncertainty by giving the DM a better
estimate of the various possibilities open to him.

Decision-Maker Uncertainties

The uncertainties with which a DM must cope at any given
time can be classified into three categories: state of
nature uncertainty, executional uncertainty, and goal uncertainty. The states of nature encompass the uncontrollable
external conditions that will determine the various outcomes.
Depending upon the decision to be made, they might include
for example weather, economy, competitive environment, gov-
ernmental regulation. The more knowledgeable the DM is of
the probable current environmental conditions (i.e., the
prevailing state of nature), the more effectively he can make
decisions.

Executional uncertainty appears in two ways. First the
DM must identify the c.o.a.'s available to him - his options.
Second, he must determine likely outcomes for each c.o.a.
under consideration. If any of five outcomes, for example,
is possible for a given c.o.a., then what is the probability
that a particular one will occur? The DM must determine
these probabilities of occurrence of various outcomes for
each c.o.a. This represents his best approximation to the
actual situation. For any complex system, the relationship
between outcomes and courses of action is probabilistic and
not deterministic even if the state of nature were known with
certainty. In other words, executional uncertainty is an

inherent part of the decision-making process.

Lastly, goal uncertainty relates outcomes to goal-achievement. The DM must examine each outcome considered and evaluate it in light of his goals: i.e., he must (if he is to be successful) recognize the value or lack thereof of each possible outcome to the attainment of his particular goals.

Each of the uncertainties discussed has both a structural and relational context. The DM has structural uncertainty about the *number* of relevant states of nature, the *number* of viable alternatives, and the *number* of outcomes that may occur as a result of executing the alternatives. Any structural deficiency will degrade the DM's performance; e.g., not considering a certain c.o.a. or not knowing that a given outcome may result will exascerbate the difference between the DM's expected and actual performance.

Once the structure is identified by the DM, he must then resolve *relational* uncertainties. What is the probability a given state of nature prevails? What is the probability that a particular c.o.a. will result in a specific outcome? What is the value of each outcome relative to goal attainment?

Some Examples

Let us now illustrate typical decision situations and specifically identify the uncertainties facing the DM.

Consider first the case of a family physician, the decision-maker. His decisions relate to proper diagnosis and treatment of the ailments of his patients. An ill patient visits his physician with a set of symptoms. The physician's first step is to identify as best he can the illness giving rise to these symptoms. The illness is the prevailing state of nature. Inasmuch as many diseases may have overlapping symptoms and give rise to the set of those symptoms experienced by the patient, identification of the specific illness clearly is probabilistic.

The next step is to identify a treatment - the course of action. Each treatment will have a number of effects, most of which are known to the physician only probabilistically - *even if he knew with certainty the precise illness* (state of nature). For example, a particular medicine may have unexpected side effects. Instead of curing the patient new symptoms may appear or old ones may be exascerbated. This is executional uncertainty.

The symptoms are given a value structure by the doctor (and by the patient also). Some symptoms are obviously of little interest, and some are vital to patient health. Note that the symptoms are the *only* observables. When the symptoms are measured, they become data and perhaps information. Blood pressure, for example, is a physical manifestation, whereas it becomes data when measured. Further examination of the patient provides information to the physician concerning the actual effects of the treatment in comparison with the expected effects, and if these differ a new course of action may now be chosen and executed thus repeating the entire process. This illustrates the feedback involved. Note that this iterative process is the only way a physician as a DM can learn more about the entire situation and in particular the effectiveness of various treatments.

A second example of some current interest which illustrates our model and corresponding uncertainties involved is that of the economy of the United States. The observables are the rate of inflation, unemployment, growth of the GNP, money supply, etc. The states of nature are inflation, recession, growth rate, energy availability, etc. These are clearly all probabilistic in nature and of course, never known with certainty at any time. In order to achieve some goal, which may be a specific growth rate or a reduced unemployment or a stable economy, certain courses of action are taken by the Government, the DM. More money may be made available to consumers by lowering taxes, a Government-financed job program may be undertaken, interest rates may be changed, etc. The relationships of these courses of action to the observables is probabilistic, and economists can speak only in terms of probabilities of certain actions having certain observable outcomes. This is, of course, the executional uncertainty which *exists even if the state of nature were known with certainty*. The goal structure is, of course, important and changeable. For example, does the President want to control inflation or cut unemployment? Which is more important (has the higher value structure)?

The outcomes are measured periodically and the results (now data) are reported to the President who examines the observable outcomes in comparison with the predicted outcomes. This is feedback. On the basis of his knowledge of the situation (his predicted model) and the data obtained, he readjusts his expectations and may choose a new course of action, and thus he reiterates the process. Again note that this iterative process is the only way to learn about the entire situation and the effectiveness of various courses of action.

Model Representation

This decision-making process can be analytically modeled in a number of different ways. One procedure that appears to represent this situation well and which can be formally manipulated uses decision matrices as shown in Figure 2. These matrices are both of dimension m by n to correspond to the m alternatives and n outcomes under consideration by the DM. An additional dimension should be added to each matrix (e.g., m by n by r) to express the r possible states of nature. Extending the model to consider other states of nature is straightforward and appears to add little to the discussion herein, so for simplicity we consider only one state of nature in the remainder of this paper. We define the matrices W and V to be the *decision state* of the DM. The decision state relates to a particular decision, is unique to each DM, and will change with time.

The W matrix describes the DM's executional uncertainty. Element w_{ij} represents the DM's *estimate* of the probability that execution of the $i\text{-}th$ alternative will result in the $j\text{-}th$ outcome. We denote by W^* the matrix describing the actual probabilities for the executional uncertainty of the decision situation. Each element w^*_{ij} of matrix W^* represents the *actual* probability of occurrence of outcome j if alternative i were to be executed. This is an *aposteriori* probability in the standard sense and represents the fraction of times outcome j would occur if alternative i were executed many times. We repeat that these matrices as indicated are for a single state of nature. There would in reality be a third dimension of dimensionality r for the different states of nature.

The decision-maker develops his estimates of the w_{ij}'s on the basis of experience and whatever data or information he has available. These are his best estimates of the w^*_{ij}'s. The more "expert" the DM is the closer his w_{ij}'s should be to the w^*_{ij}'s.

If $w_{ij} = w^*_{ij} \; \forall \; i,j$, then the DM has correctly assessed the consequence of his possible actions. If $m < m^*$, then the DM is unaware of certain courses of action; if $n < n^*$, then one or more outcomes may occur of which the DM is unaware. If $m > m^*$, then the decision-maker believes that certain

W, Probability Matrix for
outcomes for various
courses of action

Outcomes

	o_1	o_2	$\cdots$	o_n
a_1	w_{11}	w_{12}	$\cdots$	w_{1n}
a_2	w_{21}	w_{22}	$\cdots$	w_{2n}
.	.	.		.
.	.	.		.
.	.	.		.
a_m	w_{m1}	w_{m2}	$\cdots$	w_{mn}

Courses of Action

V, Value Matrix for
outcomes for various
alternatives

Outcomes

	o_1	o_2	$\cdots$	o_n
a_1	v_{11}	v_{12}	$\cdots$	v_{1n}
a_2	v_{21}	v_{22}	$\cdots$	v_{2n}
.	.	.		.
.	.	.		.
.	.	.		.
a_m	v_{m1}	v_{m2}	$\cdots$	v_{mn}

Courses of Action

Figure 2: W and V: The Decision State for
One State of Nature

courses of action are viable when in fact they are not. Similarly for $n > n^*$. We see that $w_{ij} \neq w^*_{ij}$ for some i,j suggests a *relational* uncertainty; $n \neq n^*$ or $m \neq m^*$ indicates *structural* uncertainty.

There is a *value* for every possible alternative-outcome pair. Therefore a value matrix V, also of size m by n, can be superimposed over the decision matrix W. Each element v_{ij} of matrix V represents the DM's estimate of the value of outcome j as a result of executing alternative i. Note that the value is a function not only of the outcome but also of the course of action chosen. The following examples illustrate why this must be so.

Consider the situation where a document from a collection is chosen on some basis to be relevant or non-relevant (the c.o.a.). If it is chosen to be relevant and it turns out to be relevant (the outcome), then the set of {c.o.a., outcome} has a particular value to the DM. If, on the other hand, the document were chosen to be non-relevant and it turns out to be relevant, then the value to the DM of this set is quite different from the previous situation and is in fact negative.

Consider the simple betting game of flipping a coin (heads or tails). The value matrix (if we win or lose a silver dollar) is as follows:

		Heads	Tails	{outcomes
Alternative	{Heads	$1	-$1	
	Tails	-$1	+$1	Value Matrix

Clearly the outcome values depend upon the alternative selected.

Consider also a three alternative model where the options are to buy, sell, or hold a given stock. The outcomes are that the stock price goes up, down, or remains the same. Presume that the first outcome occurs: i.e., the stock price increases. Considering our three alternatives, we observe the following: had the DM purchased some of this stock he would have realized a profit; had he sold some of this stock he would have realized a loss; had he done nothing he would have realized neither profit nor loss. Hence we see three values for the same outcome; each is alternative-dependent.

Currently for simplicity we assume $V = V^*$, where V^* denotes the actual value matrix: i.e., the DM correctly knows the value of each outcome identified. Removing this assumption adds another dimension to DM learning. Full generality, as we have indicated, considers V to be of size m by n by r for the r possible states of nature. It follows then that the value of an outcome depends also upon the existing state of nature, which may change with time.

We have chosen to use an expected value model for evaluation of the matrices. By this we mean that the expected value of any c.o.a. is computed as the weighted average of the outcome-value pairs. Given the W and V matrices which describe the decision state of the DM, one can compute the DM's expected value of each alternative as follows:

$$EV_i = \sum_{j=1}^{m} w_{ij}\, v_{ij} \tag{1}$$

Other procedures for determining values of c.o.a.'s can be used, but the expected value model is reasonable and tractable and thus convenient to use.

The m EV's computed represent the DM's *assessment* of the expected values of the m alternatives. The *actual expected value* of each alternative we denote by EV^*_i. This value is obtained by using elements w^*_{ij} of matrix W^* for the DM's w_{ij} values in equation (1) above. The EV^*_i then represents the average outcome value which would be expected if alternative i were executed many times. The DM does not know the value of EV^*_i; else he would simply choose the alternative with the highest EV^* and thus maximize his returns. The closer the DM's EV vector is to vector EV^*, the more correct his assessment of the situation and the better decision maker he should be.

Our current model considers only positive EV values: $\forall i,\ EV_i \geq 0$. We would also like to treat negative expected values for the following reason: the DM must be penalized for choosing a bad alternative. Hence his outcome value for this alternative must be negative. as indicated in the relevant/non-relevant document example described earlier. If enough executions of alternative k will result in a loss to the DM, then the resultant EV_k will be negative. Negative terms in our formulations cause certain mathematical problems which must be treated. We plan. in the near future, to expand our model so that negative EV's can be considered and handled by the model.

Making a Decision

The DM makes a decision by selecting a course of action to execute. Just how should he make this decision? Clearly it will be based upon all the data he has stored regarding his current assessment of the decision state: the W and V matrices. We have just shown how an expected value vector, EV, can be derived from the decision state. If the DM is to make a *rational* decision, then it must be based upon these data. Although we do not impose a specific decision strategy upon the DM, we will make one reasonable assumption. This is that the DM will prefer alternative i to alternative j if $EV_i > EV_j$.

The DM must establish a probability for choosing each c.o.a. In classic expected value decision theory, the DM will *always* choose the c.o.a. with the greatest expected value. But selecting the alternative of highest EV is generally the best strategy only if the DM has virtually full confidence in his derived EV values. The DM may have considerable structural or relational uncertainty regarding the situation. Also, he may wish to learn more about the total decision situation. The only way he can do this is to sample c.o.a.'s in addition to the one with maximum EV. Then he can compare predicted and observed outcomes to learn and re-evaluate his EV estimates. Furthermore, the situation may be changing with time and the DM simply may not wish to rely completely upon his previously computed EV values.

Thus we desire a method by which a probability can be associated with each alternative. representing the DM's *probability* of *selecting* that alternative. This distribution should have the properties that:

a) $\displaystyle\sum_{i=1}^{m} P(a_i) = 1;$

b) $EV_i > EV_j => P(a_i) \geq P(a_j);$

c) no DM confidence in his knowledge of

EV's $=> \forall_i\ P(a_i) = \dfrac{1}{m}\ ;$ that is, with no

information about the values to be expected, the DM will select a c.o.a. at random;

d)   total DM confidence in his knowledge of
EV's => $P(a_i) = 1$ for maximum EV_i and zero

for all others.

We propose the selection rule

$$P(a_i) = (EV_i)^C / \sum_{k=1}^{m} (EV_k)^C \quad \ni C \text{ is a non-negative real} \quad (2)$$

for situations involving positive EV values.

The variable C in equation (2) above is called the confidence factor: the higher the value of C, the higher the DM's confidence in his knowledge of the EV's. If $C = 0$ then $P(a_i) = 1/m \; \forall i$ and we have the random case. The DM has no confidence in his current state of knowledge so he prefers to make a random choice rather than let his EV's determine which c.o.a. to execute. At the other extreme, $C => \infty$ results in the classic decision theory rule: the alternative with highest EV is executed every time.

The following lemma formally demonstrates that this selection rule does indeed satisfy the four essential criteria noted above.

<u>Lemma 1</u>:   The selection rule $P(a_i) = (EV_i)^C / \sum_{k=1}^{m} (EV_k)^C$

for C, $EV_i \geq 0$ satisfies the four requisite properties for establishing the DM selection distribution.

<u>Proof</u>:

a) $\sum_{i=1}^{m} P(a_i) = 1.$

Let $P(a_i)$ be defined as in equation (2).

Then $\sum_{i=1}^{m} P(a_i) = \sum_{i=1}^{m} \left[(EV_i)^C / \sum_{k=1}^{m} (EV_k)^C \right].$

Hence $\sum_{i=1}^{m} P(a_i) = \sum_{i=1}^{m} (EV_i)^C / \sum_{k=1}^{m} (EV_k)^C = 1.$

b) $EV_i > EV_j => P(a_i) \geq P(a_j)$.

Let $EV_i > EV_j$.

Then $(EV_i)^C \geq (EV_j)^C \quad \ni C \geq 0$.

Hence $(EV_i)^C \left/ \sum\limits_{k=1}^{m} (EV_k)^C \right. \geq (EV_j)^C \left/ \sum\limits_{k=1}^{m} (EV_k)^C \right.;$

     i.e., $P(a_i) \geq P(a_j)$.

c)   No DM confidence in his knowledge of

EV's $=> \forall_i \; P(a_i) = \dfrac{1}{m}$.

Let $C = 0$.

Then we have $\forall_i \; P(a_i) = (EV_i)^0 \left/ \sum\limits_{k=1}^{m} (EV_k)^0 \right.$.

Hence $\forall_i \; P(a_i) = 1 \left/ \sum\limits_{k=1}^{m} 1 \right. = \dfrac{1}{m}$.

d)   Total DM confidence in his knowledge of

EV's $=> \exists \; i \ni P(a_i) = 1$ and all other $P(a_k) = 0$.

Assume $\exists \; i \ni \forall_k \; EV_i > EV_k$ for $i \neq k$.

Then consider the term $P(a_i)$ as $C \to \infty$.

$$\lim_{C \to \infty} P(a_i) = \lim_{C \to \infty} \left[(EV_i)^C \left/ \sum\limits_{k=1}^{m} (EV_k)^C \right. \right]$$

$$= \lim_{C \to \infty} \left\{ 1 \left/ \left[\sum\limits_{k=1}^{m} (EV_k)^C \left/ (EV_i)^C \right. \right] \right. \right\}$$

$$= \lim_{C \to \infty} \left\{ 1 \left/ \sum\limits_{k=1}^{m} \left[(EV_k)^C \left/ (EV_i)^C \right. \right] \right. \right\} .$$

But $\forall k \neq i \; \lim\limits_{C \to \infty} (EV_k)^C \left/ (EV_i)^C \right. = \lim\limits_{C \to \infty} (EV_k / EV_i)^C = 0,$

since $EV_i > EV_k$.

Lastly, for $k = i$ $\lim\limits_{C \to \infty} (EV_k)^C / (EV_i)^C$

$$= \lim\limits_{C \to \infty} \left(\frac{EV_k}{EV_i}\right)^C = \lim\limits_{C \to \infty} \left(\frac{1}{1}\right)^C = 1.$$

Therefore $\lim\limits_{C \to \infty} P(a_i) = 1$ and by a) above,

$$\forall k \neq i \quad \lim\limits_{C \to \infty} P(a_k) = 0.$$

QED

Decision-Maker Learning

In our approach, we use equations (1) and (2) in order to calculate Expected Values and Probabilities of alternatives available to the DM. The following sequence of events then occurs. This procedure is a general one for all expected value models and is not dependent upon specific formulations of the probabilities. In actual practice, the DM may determine probabilities mainly by judgment rather than from calculation.

1. DM estimates or predicts EV_i for $i = 1, 2, \ldots, m$ on the basis of all of his past experiences using equation (1);

2. DM establishes $P(a_i)$ for $i = 1, 2, \ldots, m$ from his estimates of the EV_i and his current level of confidence in the data. In our approach he uses equation (2) to derive these estimates;

3. DM now executes an alternative, k, in accordance with his estimates of the probabilities developed in step 2;

4. Given the prevailing state of nature, some outcome occurs as a result of executing alternative k. Remember that the DM is only probabilistically knowledgeable about which outcome will occur.

5. The resultant outcome is now fed back to the DM in accordance with Figure 1, permitting the DM to upgrade his assessment of the situation.

6. On the basis of this feedback information the DM updates his estimate of EV_k and his assessment of the probabilities of the outcomes for that alternative. Note that the DM's assessment of the decision situation and all the

values thereof are a function of his previous experience and the data obtained from the decisions he has made.

7. Go back to step 2, update the P's using the new EV_k and continue.

Step 6 in the above characterization of DM activity, using feedback data to update the DM's state of knowledge (or decision state), is what we call "relational learning". This learning can be considered to be effected by making row changes to the W matrix. Or, in a more macroscopic sense, we simply alter the current EV assessment corresponding to the alternative executed. In either case (macro or micro) the end result is an updated DM estimate of EV_k. No other EV's are altered since only one c.o.a. has been executed; the feedback data clearly relates only to the alternative executed. Of course from equation (2) we note that all his probabilities are altered due to a change in one EV and/or a change in his confidence.

Learning can be modeled by adjusting the DM's expected value of the alternative just executed. The value of the observed outcome is averaged into the DM's EV approximation in some way. A number of learning rules could be used to update the EV's. We have, for convenience, chosen the following learning rule inasmuch as it does seem to be descriptive of the actual process. In this situation c.o.a. k has been executed at time t resulting in the actual value $V_k(t)$ occurring. The DM then updates his old estimate of the expected value for c.o.a. k by

$$EV_k(t+1) = [1-\lambda_k(t)] \; EV_k(t) + \lambda_k(t) \; V_k(t), \quad 0 \le \lambda \le 1. \quad (3)$$

That is, the expected value of alternative k at time $t+1$ is simply a weighted average of the expected value at time t and the actual outcome value obtained at time t, $V_k(t)$.

The learning parameter λ should be a decreasing function of time and confidence. For instance, a possible definition of $\lambda_k(t)$ might be:

$$\lambda_k(t) = 1/[(C_k+1) \times number \; of \; trials \; for \; c.o.a. \; k]. \quad (4)$$

Variable C_k is the DM's confidence factor in his estimation of EV_k and goes from 0 to infinity.

Note that when the DM has little confidence in his estimates, or when he has little data on which to base an estimate, his learning will be large (almost one) and when his confidence is high the learning will be small (almost zero).

Two important aspects of this learning algorithm should be noted. First, it should be clear that learning causes a chain reaction: altering a row of the W matrix alters the respective EV which in turn alters the DM's probabilities for selecting an alternative (by our selection rule).

Second, the DM's confidence plays an important role in both learning and selection. Although the parameter, confidence, is used in both equation (2) for selection procedure and equation (4) for learning, the two may differ inasmuch as they describe different phenomena. Furthermore, in equation (2) the variable C is an *overall* confidence in the entire situation, whereas in equation (4) the variable C_k applies to the confidence that a DM has in his knowledge of the outcome of a particular c.o.a. Further research on this matter, both conceptual and experimental, is underway.

The Basic Information Measure

Given our model of information flow and analysis, we can now develop definitions of important terms which can then be quantified and measured and which are of course consistent with the basic theory. We first define our fundamental measure of information from the standpoint of effectiveness. All levels of information have one important point in common: information reduces some uncertainty. Uncertainty in the effectiveness sense should relate to the DM's choice of a c.o.a. How certain is the DM about which alternative should be chosen?

The uncertainty in choosing a course of action clearly relates directly to the DM's probabilities of executing each course of action. For example, if all of the probabilities are the same, then the DM is totally uncertain which alternative should be selected. At the other extreme, if the DM is completely certain as to his course of action then for some i, $P(a_i) = 1$ and all of the other probabilities are zero. Thus we choose the *variance* of the P's as a basis for our measure of information. Note that the variance is zero when all of the P's are the same and a maximum when one P is unity and the others are zero.

The mean square variance of the probabilities, $\sigma^2(P)$, is by definition:

$$\sigma^2(P) = \sum_{i=1}^{m} [P(a_i) - \mu(P)]^2/m, \qquad (5)$$

and the mean, $\mu(P)$, is:

$$\mu(P) = \left[\sum_{i=1}^{m} P(a_i)\right]/m = \frac{1}{m}, \qquad (6)$$

where m is the number of viable courses of action.

Any basic measure of information should possess a number of fundamental properties. First, it should be defined in terms of some fundamental unit of measure. It should be at a maximum when the variance of the elements is maximal, and it should be at a minimum when the variance is minimal. These bounds should be well defined. The measure should be indifferent to the order of consideration of the elements. It must be stable; i.e., the consideration of an additional c.o.a. of low probability should not have a significant effect upon the measure. Finally, the measure should be sequentially additive. Whether applied once to the entire set of elements or respectively to a set of mutually exclusive and exhaustive subsets, the measure should yield the same result. A measure of information which possesses the aforementioned properties would provide a sound basis for our theory of effective information.

We have indicated that any effectiveness measure of information must relate to the variance of the DM's probabilities of selection of the alternatives. However, it is not the variance directly but the normalized variance which is important. The simplest way to consider the variance of a population in a normalized form is to divide it by the square of the mean, that is to consider the r.m.s. deviation in terms of units of the mean. It is clear that we must consider a normalized variance since a given variance about the mean will be much less significant when the mean is large than when the mean is small.

Hence we define our fundamental measure of information to be:

$$I = \sigma^2(P)/\mu^2(P). \qquad (7)$$

Since $\mu^2(P) = 1/m^2$ (see equation (6)), we observe that this measure relates the variance to m, the number of courses of action.

Referring to equations (5), (6), and (7), we see that

$$I = \sigma^2(P)/\mu^2(P) = \left[\sum_{i=1}^{m}\left(P(a_i) - \frac{1}{m}\right)^2 / m\right] \Big/ \left(\frac{1}{m}\right)^2$$

$$= m \sum_{i=1}^{m} P(a_i)^2 - 1 .$$

This quantity possesses the desired properties for an information measure as we now demonstrate. Thus, we define this
quantity to be *the amount of information in the decision
state*, viz

$$I = m \sum_{i=1}^{m} P(a_i)^2 - 1 . \tag{8}$$

Properties of Information Measure

The information measure as defined possesses most of the
desired properties of a fundamental measure of information
effectiveness.

This quantity has a minimum of zero when all the $P(a_i)$'s
are equal to $\frac{1}{m}$ (pure chance). This is complete uncertainty.
The quantity has a maximum of $m - 1$ in the case of complete
certainty where one of the $P(a_i)$'s is one and the others are
zero.

When there are only two possible courses of action, the
quantity I will assume values from zero to one. It will be
equal to one under condition of certainty, i.e., when the
probability of choosing one course of action is one and the
other probability is zero. Accordingly, we will define the
unit of information in terms of a deterministic two-choice
situation. This unit we call a *binary choice unit*, or b.c.u.

When there are m possible courses of action, then the
maximum amount of information from equation (8) is seen to be
$m - 1$ b.c.u.'s. This is in agreement with a well-known
combinatoric principle that a minimum of $m - 1$ deterministic
choices from pairs of alternatives is required when there
are m alternatives to consider. More explicitly, if $m - 1$
choices are required and the maximum amount of information in
each choice is one, then the maximum amount of information is
$m - 1$. Analogously the minimum amount of information is
zero.

Clearly the measure is indifferent to the order in which the elements are considered. Since addition is associative, the P's can be summed in any order yielding a unique result. Hence the alternatives can be considered in any order.

The consideration of additional courses of action of low probability have an insignificant effect upon the measure. This is seen from equation (8) inasmuch as the sum of the P^2 will be essentially unchanged with the addition of such a c.o.a. However, the m will change by one and thus the relative information change is proportional to $\frac{1}{m}$. Thus the addition of a new c.o.a. does not *significantly* alter I for reasonable size m.

An additional question to be considered is the additivity of our measure. The measure itself clearly does not possess simple linear additivity since it is based on a non-linear distribution, e.g., the variance. This must be the case inasmuch as the probability of choosing any course of action must depend on *all* the other courses of action. However, the measure does have an important additivity property involving expected values.

The probability of choosing any course of action is a function of the decision-maker's expectation of all the values as we have seen in equation (2). The values (or the expectation of the values) on the other hand are independent of each other. We show below that the values of subsets of the courses of action are indeed additive and can be considered separately. Thus in going from the values to the probabilities to information we show an important additivity property. Hence the decision-maker's estimate of performance (defined in equation (12) below) for disjoint subsets A, B of the courses of action has the following additivity property:

The DM's estimate of performance with sets (A, B) equals his estimate of performance for set (A) multiplied by the probability of selecting set (A) plus his estimate of performance for set (B) multiplied by the probability of selecting set (B). Thus in order to add information in disjoint sets we must first consider the fundamental values.

The proof of this statement follows:

Consider set S of alternatives a_1, a_2, ..., a_m and its associated EV_i and $P_S(a_i)$ for $i = 1, 2, ..., m$. Then by definition from equation (12) below

$$DP_S = \sum_{i=1}^{m} P_S(a_i)\ EV_i\ .$$

Now consider a partitioning of S into disjoint subsets A and B whose union is S. As order of evaluation for DP_S is unimportant, rename the alternatives so that a_1, a_2, ..., $a_k \in A$ and a_{k+1}, a_{k+2}, ..., $a_m \in B$. Now consider computing DP_A: note that $\sum_{i=1}^{k} P_S(a_i) \neq 1$, since

$k < m$. If only these alternatives are to be considered, then they must be factored uniformly so that they sum to 1. Hence we set $P_A(a_i) = P_S(a_i) / \sum_{j=1}^{k} P_S(a_j)$, which uniformly increases the probabilities for alternatives in $A \ni \sum_{i=1}^{k} P_A(a_i) = 1$.

Thus $DP_A = \sum_{i=1}^{k} P_A(a_i)\ EV_i = \sum_{i=1}^{k} \left[P_S(a_i)\ EV_i \ / \ \sum_{j=1}^{k} P_S(a_j) \right].$

A similar term is derived for set B; i.e.,

$$DP_B = \sum_{i=k+1}^{m} P_B(a_i)\ EV_i = \sum_{i=k+1}^{m} \left[P_S(a_i)\ EV_i \ / \ \sum_{j=k+1}^{m} P_S(a_j) \right].$$

If a DM now wishes to combine these two evaluations to consider all m alternatives collectively, then it is only natural to consider the sets A and B as two alternative sets with associated probabilities of selection $P(A)$ and $P(B)$ and estimated values DP_A and DP_B. Thus,

$DP_{A \cup B} = P(A) \times DP_A + P(B) \times DP_B.$ But

$P(A) = \sum_{i=1}^{k} P_S(a_i)$ and $P(B) = \sum_{i=k+1}^{m} P_S(a_i).$ So substituting

$P(A)$, $P(B)$, DP_A and DP_B into our equality, we have

$$DP_{AUB} = \sum_{i=1}^{k} P_S(a_i) \left[\sum_{i=1}^{k} P_S(a_i) \, EV_i \, / \sum_{j=1}^{k} P_S(a_j) \right] +$$

$$\sum_{i=k+1}^{m} P_S(a_i) \left[\sum_{i=k+1}^{m} P_S(a_i) \, EV_i \, / \sum_{j=k+1}^{m} P_S(a_j) \right]$$

$$= \sum_{i=1}^{m} P_S(a_i) \, EV_i = DP_S \, .$$

QED

Amount of Information in a Data Set

A measure of the amount of information in a data set or message can be arrived at by computing the difference in the amount of information in the decision state after and before receipt of the data. That is, the amount of information is determined by considering the impact these new data have on the decision-maker's decision state. In symbolic terms, $I(D)$, *the amount of information in data set D*, is

$$I(D) = I_{t+1} - I_t \, , \tag{9}$$

where I_{t+1} and I_t are the amounts of information in the decision state after and before receipt of the data set.

It should be noted that the amount of information in a data set may be either positive or negative. In general, positive information sharpens or refines the decision-maker's understanding of the situation in that it either reduces the number of structural components in the model or reduces the dispersion in one or more of the various probability distributions in the model. Negative information, on the other hand, either increases the number of structural components (e.g., the addition to the model of a previously unknown alternative or outcome) or increases the dispersion in the various distributions. Negative information, despite a possible connotation of the term, does represent information that is of significance to the decision-maker.

This measure will in general vary with time; it will in general differ with different DM's and with different situations. This variation is consistent with the fact that data cannot be evaluated out of context. For instance, a given document which is relevant to a scientist working on a problem in nuclear physics is probably non-relevant to an

economist. Knowing next month's projected output is of value
to a DM worried about finding buyers or projecting future
output, but after that month has passed the DM will use the
actual output data, not the old projections. Lastly, each
DM is different and thus may react differently to the same
data; hence a different $I(D)$. This is a measure personal to
the DM that is time and situation dependent.

Related Measures

We have now defined a quantitative measure of the
amount of information in terms of the fundamental unit,
b.c.u. From an effectiveness standpoint, we are further
concerned with the *value* of the information. In order to
establish a measure of the value of information, we first
must define a term which describes the capability of a
decision maker to achieve his goals. Such a term we will
call decision-maker effectiveness or *DME*. We can then define
the *value* of information in terms of the corresponding change
in the *DME*. This will then be a measure of the effectiveness
with which the DM uses the information available to him.

We will define *DME* in terms of the average expected
performance of the DM at any given time. The DM executes the
c.o.a.'s in accordance with his probability distribution.
The *average* outcome of alternative i is EV_i^*, the actual
expected value. Thus, average DM performance, AP, can be
expressed as:

$$AP = \sum_{i=1}^{m} P(a_i) \ EV_i^* \ . \tag{10}$$

If the DM makes a series of decisions with these probabilities, then his performance, *on the average*, will be that
projected by AP. Actual DM performance at time t is a
specific value $V_k(t)$ which is obtained from the alternative
executed, a_k. Note that $V_k(t)$ will in fact be one of v_{kj}'s
associated with alternative k as seen from observation of
Figure 2. The values obtained by execution of c.o.a., a_k,
will vary according to the probabilities defined by the
starred matrix and will vary about the mean EV_k^* with a
variance determined by the values and their probabilities.
Observation of each row of the value matrix indicates the
extreme values.

Because of the fluctuations possible in *actual* DM performance, we define the decision-maker effectiveness in terms of the *average* DM performance as compared to the maximum possible DM performance. The maximum possible DM performance occurs when $max\ EV_k^*$ is chosen with certainty. Thus

$$DME = AP/max(EV_k^*),$$

$$DME = \sum_{i=1}^{m} P(a_i)\ (EV_i^*)/max(EV_k^*). \qquad (11)$$

DME is a dimensionless unit which goes from zero to one and tells us how well the DM is able to meet his goals. Note that *AP* is clearly additive in the same way as we showed above for *DP*, the DM's estimate of his performance.

A rational DM should increase his *DME* with time on the average, as $max\ (EV_k^*)$ is constant and average performance $(\Sigma P(a_i)\ EV_i^*)$ should increase as feedback data enhances the DM's probabilities of choice, $P(a_i)$. We see that if $P(a_k) = 1$ for the maximum valued EV_k^*, then *DME = 1*, the maximum.

Of course, the DM does not know the EV^*'s with certainty. He can only approximate them probabilistically. Therefore, the DM can only estimate his *DME* and, in fact, his best approximation to his performance is given by the term we define to be the DM expected performance, *DP*. That is

$$DP = \sum_i P(a_i)\ EV_i , \qquad (12)$$

where EV_i is the DM's estimate of EV_i^*. As the DM becomes more expert, his *DP* approaches *AP*.

The DM does not know the $max\ EV^*$ and therefore he can only estimate his *DME* from equation (12). This would take the form of *DP* divided by his estimate of the maximum (EV_i).

Every decision maker has a perception of his own effectiveness for a given situation. We are interested empirically in relating the DM's estimate of his effectiveness to that calculated from our equations above for *DME* and *DP*. We are planning both simulations and experiments to determine the similarity of these two terms.

Value of Information

Decision-maker effectiveness, as defined in equation (11), provides the basis for our measure of the *value* of information, $Q(D)$. As our measures are concerned with the effectiveness level of information, it is natural to define the value of information to be related to its effect upon the performance of the DM. Did the new data increase or decrease the DM's performance, and by how much?

Because of the variations possible in actual DM performance at a given time, we believe it is only meaningful to consider the performance on an *average* basis. This, of course, is accompanied with a mean square deviation, σ^2 about the average. Hence $DME_{t+1} - DME_t$ would show the change in DM effectiveness (see equation 11) due to information received. Thus we define $Q(D)$, *the value of the information in data set D*, as:

$$Q(D) = DME_{t+1} - DME_t . \tag{13}$$

The measure DME is well defined and ranges from 0 to 1; hence our value measure $Q(D)$ ranges from -1 to +1. Data that results in decreased DM performance are of negative information value; if they do not effect performance, then they are of no value, and $Q(D) = 0$.

The value measure $Q(D)$ is described in terms of a basic unit: DME. It has prescribed upper and lower bounds that are consistant with the intended meaning of $Q(D)$. The measure is associative and additive if the AP is considered directly. Thus, this measure, $Q(D)$, possesses all of the properties we require of a fundamental information measure.

Hence we have developed two fundamental metrics which measure *information amount, I(D)*, and *information value, Q(D)*. While the quantity $I(D)$ shows the change in the DM's plans for dealing with the situation, the quantity $Q(D)$ defines the value accrued from the DM's change in probabilities. These two measures are thus distinct, yet they are interdependent. However, the relationship between them is quite complex. Information amount deals with the DM's actions; information value relates to DM performance. Further research will determine under what assumptions general relationships can be guaranteed.

Summary of Definitions

In this paper we have developed a number of important definitions characterizing information and decision-making. This section reviews those definitions so that they can be considered together in a meaningful manner. We list each term, describe its meaning, and repeat its definition as given previously.

a) <u>Expected Value</u> of a c.o.a., a_i: the expected value of an alternative is the weighted average of the outcome values.

$$EV_i = \sum_{j=1}^{m} w_{ij} \, v_{ij} \, . \tag{1}$$

b) <u>Selection Rule</u> for c.o.a.'s: the probability of selecting alternative i is proportional to its relative expected value raised to the DM's confidence.

$$P(a_i) = (EV_i)^C / \sum_{k=1}^{m} (EV_k)^C \, . \tag{2}$$

c) <u>Learning Rule</u> for expected value of c.o.a. (a_k): the new expected value of alternative k, given the outcome value of a prior execution, is a weighted combination of the old expected value and the observed outcome value.

$$EV_k(t+1) = [1-\lambda_k(t)] \, EV_k(t) + \lambda_k(t) \, V_k \, . \tag{3}$$

d) <u>Information in the Decision State</u>: the amount of information in the decision state of the DM in $b.c.u.$'s is

$$I = m \sum_{i=1}^{m} P(a_i)^2 - 1 \, . \tag{8}$$

e) <u>Information Amount</u>: the amount of information in a data set D is defined as the change in the information of the DM's decision state after and before receipt of the data.

$$I(D) = I_{t+1} - I_t \, . \tag{9}$$

f) <u>DM Actual Performance</u>: actual DM performance at time t is the actual value of outcome j, which is obtained from the alternative executed, a_k:

$$DM\ actual\ performance\ (t)\ =\ V_k(t)\ =\ v_{kj}\ .$$

g) <u>DM Average Performance</u>: the average performance of a DM is the weighted average of the actual expected outcome values.

$$AP\ =\ \sum_{i=1}^{m}\ P(a_i)\ EV_i^{*}\ . \tag{10}$$

h) <u>Decision-maker Effectiveness</u>: the effectiveness of a DM is the ratio of his average performance to the maximum expected outcome value.

$$DME\ =\ \sum_{i=1}^{m}\ P(a_i)\ (EV_i^{*})/max(EV_k^{*})\ . \tag{11}$$

i) <u>DM Expected Performance</u>: the DM's estimate of his average performance is the weighted average of his expected outcome values.

$$DP\ =\ \sum_{i=1}^{m}\ P(a_i)\ EV_i\ . \tag{12}$$

j) <u>Information Value</u>: the value of the information in a data set D to a given DM is defined to be his change in effectiveness.

$$Q(D)\ =\ DME_{t+1}\ -\ DME_t\ . \tag{13}$$

Conclusions and Further Research

The fundamental goal of this research is to develop a comprehensive, usable theory of information at the effectiveness level. Thus far we have defined a detailed model for information flow and analysis. We have suggested that most decision-making situations can be modeled within this formulation. We have developed an underlying mathematical framework to define the decision state of the decision maker: matrices W and V. From this framework we have algorithmically defined procedures to model, we believe realistically, DM data assimilation, DM selection, and DM execution of alternatives. The entire model implies iteration many times so that the DM can better estimate the decision state and various associated parameters. With this framework we believe that we can accurately describe the use of

information in an effectiveness sense and the role of
information in the total decision process.

We have defined herein a number of important information-
related measures. Two of these of particular importance are
the amount of information $I(D)$ and value of information $Q(D)$,
which quantify the information in a data set D. Other
measures that can be derived from our model include the
amount of information in the decision state (I), decision-
maker effectiveness (DME), decision-maker expected performance (DP) and DM average performance (AP). These measures
provide us with a quantitative basis for analyzing and
defining information flow and for identifying limitations of
this flow.

Continuing research involves establishing relationships
among these quantities and the significance of each to the
information flow process. We are seeking generalized information relationships in an effort to establish fundamental
guidelines for information flow, analysis, storage, and
processing. In addition, we feel that generalized rules for
making decisions under various conditions - a decision
calculus - will emerge from this model as well.

We are planning to apply this theoretical development to
practical situations and indicate how the quantities can be
defined, measured, and used in a practical way. In particular, we are developing examples using a bibliographical
retrieval system, a production control situation, and a
general economic model.

Of course, of primary concern is the question of
validation in an empirical sense of our theory and measures.
We have developed a simulation model to verify some of our
basic measures and procedures and to determine their value.
Two versions of the simulation model have been implemented
in FORTRAN: a batch model and an interactive model. The
batch model is running on an IBM 370/168 and is being used
for running long repetitive decision situations with many
trials. Aggregate data from test cases are being studied to
determine if the results are consistent with the theory and
to find further relationships between the basic quantities
defined in our information flow model. The interactive model
is running on a PDP-10 and enables direct input to be made
by a human decision maker. We plan to conduct actual experiments using a document collection and real decision makers
in order to establish the various paramaters and their
validity.

References

1. Yovits, M.C., and Ernst, R.L., "Generalized Information Systems: Consequences for Information Transfer," *People and Information*, ed. by H.P. Pepinsky, Pergamon Press, New York, 1969.

2. Whittemore, B.J., and Yovits, M.C., "A Generalized Conceptual Development for the Analysis and Flow of Information," *JASIS*, May–June 1973, Vol. 24, No. 3, 221–231.

3. Yovits, M.C., and Abilock, J.G., "A Semiotic Framework for Information Science Leading to the Development of a Quantitative Measure of Information," *Information Utilities; Proceedings of the 37th ASIS Annual Meeting*, Vol. 11, Atlanta, 1974.

4. Shannon, C.E., and Weaver, W., *The Mathematical Theory of Communication*, The University of Illinois Press, Urbana, Ill., 1949.

5. Weiner, N., *The Human Use of Human Beings*, Houghton Mifflin Co., Boston, 1950.

6. Carnap, R., and Bar-Hillel, Y., "An Outline of a Theory of Semantic Information," Technical Report #247, Research Laboratory of Electronics, MIT, 1952.

7. Winograd, T., "Understanding Natural Language," *Cognitive Psychology*, 3, 1972.

8. Zunde, P., "Information Measurement and Value," *Third Annual Symposium of the American Society for Cybernetics*, Gaithersburg, Md., October 1969.

9. MacKay, D.M., *Information, Mechanism, and Meaning*, MIT Press, Cambridge, Mass., 1969.

10. Ackoff, R.L., "Towards a Behavioral Theory of Communication," *Management Science*, 4 (1958), 218–234.

11. Marshak, J., "Problems in Information Economics," *Management Controls*, ed. by C.P. Bonini, et al, McGraw-Hill, New York, 1964, 38–74.

12. MacKay, D.M., "Quantal Aspects of Scientific Information," *Philosophical Magazine*, Vol. 41, No. 314, March, 1950, 289–311.

13. Cherry, C., *On Human Communication*, MIT Press, Cambridge, Mass., 1966.

14. Goffman, W., "On the Dynamics of Communication," *AAAS Conference Proceedings*, Denver, Colorado, February 1977.

15. Morris, W.T., *The Analysis of Management Decisions*, Richard D. Irwin, Inc., Homewood, Ill., 1964.

16. Raiffa, H., *Decision Analysis, Introductory Lecture on Choices Under Uncertainty*, Addison-Wesley, Reading, Mass., 1971.

17. Schlaiffer, R., *Analysis of Decisions under Uncertainty*, McGraw-Hill, New York, 1969.

18. Radnor, R., "Normative Theory and Individual Decision - An Introduction," *Decision and Organization*, ed. by C.B. McGuire and R. Radnor, North Holland Publishing Co., Amsterdam, 1972.

19. Bandyopadhyay, R., "Information for Organizational Decisionmaking - A Literature Review," *IEEE Transactions on Systems, Man, and Cybernetics*, Vol. SMC-7, No. 1, January 1977.

3

Information Structures
in the Language
of Science

Naomi Sager

INTRODUCTION

This paper presents results, and computer applications, of research into the relation between language structure and information, particularly as it appears in the language of science.

Information is not something separate from language. It is true we convey some meanings by extralinguistic means, but for all practical purposes, the way of storing and transmitting information, and probably of forming new information, is largely via language. To study the relation between information and language, our method has been to analyze scientific writing in a systematic way, using syntactic and statistical methods which can be applied with little change to written material from many sciences.

Using the regularities observed in the language material itself, we have developed computer programs for processing the information in natural language reports and articles. The programs convert the natural language text of the input documents into table-like structures (called information formats) by aligning words which carry the same type of information into a single column. The columns of the table are defined in such a way that the syntactic relations between the words of the sentence are preserved in the table. This way, no textual information is lost, and the original sentences, or paraphrases of them, are reconstructible from the table. At the same time, this mapping of the text sentences into formats makes the information in the text accessible for further computer processing and brings it into line with information presented in other forms, such as tables published in the literature.

SIMPLE PARSE DIAGRAM

GL 641 13.6.11 CALCIUM UPTAKE INTO LIVER MITOCHONDRIA APPEARS NOT TO BE AFFECTED BY CARDIAC GLYCOSIDES.

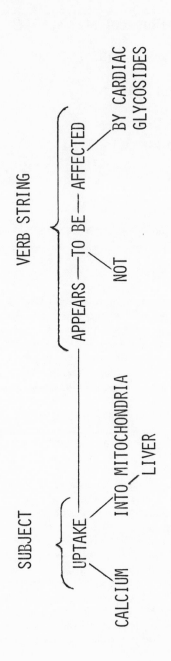

FIGURE 1

The main practical implication of these information formatting programs is that large files of technical documents on a given subject could be queried by computer for particular information, or summarized with respect to particular categories, without the necessity to code or alter the input natural language documents. A pilot experiment on radiology reports of cancer patients demonstrated that the computer system was able to transform the sentences of the English language reports into the appropriate tabular structures without loss of information, and to retrieve specific factual information from the computer-formatted reports. For each report the system was able to format the sentences of the report and from the resulting tables to answer such questions as: Was a test made (for given patient during given period)? Were the findings negative? Is there some question about the findings? When was the first metastasis reported? Where was it? and other questions (1).

It should be noted from the outset that these programs are not based upon semantic categories that are supplied beforehand by someone with knowledge of the given science. They are based on general properties of language structure and on the fact that words with similar informational standing in the science occur in similar positions vis a vis other words in the texts. We have demonstrated by means of a clustering program (to be described later) that the word classes of semantic value in a science subfield can be generated on the basis of the distributional similarity of the words in the subfield texts. For example, Ca^{++} and Na^+ are found to be in the same class in some of our texts, not because they are known to be names of ions, but because they both occur as subjects of the same type of verb in the textual material.

Computerized Language Processing

It is only possible for the computer to convert the information in science documents from their natural language form into more regular forms by building upon the regularities which are in the language material itself. These regularities exist on two levels; one common to the language as a whole and one specific to the subject matter. The regularities which obtain for a whole language are summarized in its grammar. The first stage of computer processing, then, is to analyze each input sentence as an instance of a grammatical structure, specified in a computerized grammar provided to the program. The program which does this, a so-called "parser", segments each sentence into its major grammatical components (main clause, modifiers, etc.) and shows how the components are interconnected [Figure 1]. Parsing is important not only as a first step in breaking-up a large unwieldy sentence into smaller more tractable units, but also because some of the grammatical relations recognized at this stage are themselves part of the information; to use a simple example, the relation of subject-verb-object in an assertion makes the difference between, e.g. <u>the ion enters the cell</u> and <u>the cell enters the ion</u>.

But while the parsing program provides a useful decomposition of the sentence into its grammatical components, the language provides for so very many different kinds of grammatical components that further regularization is necessary. Many grammatical forms are equivalent with regard to the substantive information they carry, for example, the active and passive forms. These equivalences can be utilized by the computer in order to reduce the number of alternative grammatical forms that have to be dealt with. The most common one among the equivalent forms is chosen as the base form and the program is equipped with procedures which transform occurrences of the equivalent forms into the base form. Very often the transformation fills out elliptical assertions into full assertions. This not only reduces the number of forms to be dealt with but regularizes the pattern of word occurrences which is important for informational alignment. As a simple example, the sentence <u>Samples of Na_2SO_4 were irradiated and analyzed</u> contains the <u>segment and analyzed</u>, consisting of <u>and</u> plus a participle. The computer eliminates this special form by expanding the segment to a full assertion, as though the sentence read: <u>Samples of Na_2SO_4 were irradiated and samples of Na_2SO_4 were analyzed</u>. From here it is a straightforward step to align corresponding parts of the assertions. In addition, in this example, the computer could reduce the two passive assertions to two active assertions with unspecified subjects: <u>Someone irradiated samples of Na_2SO_4 and someone analyzed samples of Na_2SO_4</u>. This would be useful if elsewhere in the texts active forms involving the same words occurred; but often we find that this is not the case. The so-called scientific passive serves as a better base form for much science material, especially laboratory procedures and measurements, where one wants to align both properties and procedures as predicates on the experimental material.

Sublanguage Grammars

The second type of regularity which appears in science writing is not common to the language as a whole, but is specific to the particular subfield of science from which the texts are drawn. One has to realize that journal articles and technical reports are communications between specialists who "talk the same language." Here the metaphor has literal

truth. Investigators or practitioners in a given field speak
a language which is not identical to the over-all language,
say English, even though they use English words and do not
violate English grammar. They speak a sublanguage which dif-
fers from English in several ways. It does not use the full
range of constructions permitted by the grammar of the whole
language, and it is constrained by rules that do not apply
in the language as a whole.

In the case of a whole language we know that there are
grammatical rules because some word sequences are accepted
by native speakers of the language as wellformed sentences
while other sequences are rejected as ungrammatical. A similar situation exists in a community of individuals engaged
in a specialized field of science. Certain statements will
be accepted as possible within the discipline while others
will be rejected as impossible or outlandish. I do not speak
here of truth versus falsity or even accepted versus uncon-
ventional formulations, but of statements which run counter
to common knowledge which is fundamental to the discipline.
Thus, for example, the statement <u>the ion enters the cell</u>
would be acceptable to a specialist working on cellular pro-
cesses--it may or may not be true in a given case--whereas
<u>the cell enters the ion</u> would be definitively rejected as
being not merely false but unsayable in the science. This
linguistic behavior on the part of the scientist indicates
that rules analogous to the rules of grammar for the whole
language are operating in the language of a science subfield.

It is by making explicit the regularities of language
usage on the subfield level, that we are able to construct
formats for housing the information in subfield texts. Just
as a grammar provides syntactic formulas in terms of the
classes Noun, Verb, etc., a sublanguage grammar provides analogous formulas in terms of those specific subclasses of
Noun, Verb, etc. which are characteristic of the subfield,
e.g. in cell biology, classes for ions, molecules, cell
structures, verbs of motion, verbs of cause, etc. These subclasses are found by clustering (manually, or by computer)
words with similar co-occurrence patterns <u>vis</u> <u>a</u> <u>vis</u> other
words in the texts. The sublanguage formulas are thus summaries of syntactic regularities in texts constrained by a
particular subject matter. They emerge as formats for the
textual information because of the close relation on this
level between form and meaning. Ions do only certain things;
therefore ion-words occur as the subject of only certain
verbs.

GL641 13.6.11   CALCIUM UPTAKE INTO LIVER MITOCHONDRIA APPEARS
NOT TO BE AFFECTED BY CARDIAC GLYCOSIDES.

DRUG	V-CAUSE	ARG1	V-PHYS	ARG2	CONJ
CARDIAC GLYCOSIDES	AFFECT (APPEARS NOT TO)	CALCIUM	UPTAKE INTO	MITOCHONDRIA (LIVER)	.

FIGURE 2

INFORMATION FORMATS

To illustrate what is meant by an information format for science writing, consider the formatted sentence in Figure 2. This example, and several others in this paper, are taken from a study of journal articles in a subfield of pharmacology concerned with the mechanisms of action of digitalis and other cardiac glycosides. We analyzed manually, and with the aid of the computer, some 200 journal pages in this field, and found that sublanguage formulas covering the main factual results could be stated in the form of a sublanguage grammar, and that the sublanguage grammar could be used in procedures to map the text sentences into a limited number of format structures.

Fact Units

The formats obtained in the pharmacology study contained one case or another of the basic unit illustrated in the format in Figure 2 for the sentence <u>Calcium uptake into liver mitochondria appears not to be affected by cardiac glycosides.</u> In this sentence, as in most others in this material, there is an inner, or "bottom level," assertion (shown in the format between double bars) consisting of a verb with its subject and object. In the pharmacology texts, this assertion described an elementary physiological or biochemical event, which in the case of Figure 2 is the uptake of calcium into the mitochondria of the liver. The inner assertion here is an instance of a formula that recurred over and over in these texts, $N_{ION} V_{MOVE} N_{CELL}$, in which a noun in the ion class is connected to a noun in the cell or cell substructure class by a verb in a class which expresses movement, though the class is defined by its syntactic position connecting the above two noun classes. Examples of other elementary assertions encountered in this literature were those covering ion interactions, enzyme activity, tissue contraction or contractility, protein behavior and ions binding to molecules.

Operating on the elementary assertion, very often, was a noun-verb pair, shown in Figure 2 to the left of the double bars, consisting of a drug word and a verb of roughly causal character (<u>affect</u>, <u>influence</u>, etc.) possibly negated or quantified, as in this sentence. The causal pair is said to "operate on" the elementary assertion because the latter appears as the object of the causal verb. Notice that we had to perform the regularizing transformation passive → active in order to reveal that <u>uptake</u> is the object of <u>affect</u>, since it appears in the sentence as the subject of the passive construction <u>appears not to be affected</u>. Also, while <u>uptake</u> appears in the sentence as a noun, it is in fact a

GL 641 2.2.1 MORE DETAILED STUDIES OF THE AFFECTS OF CARDIAC GLYCOSIDES
ON SODIUM AND POTASSIUM MOVEMENTS IN RED CELLS HAVE BEEN
MADE BY KAHN AND ACHESON (99), SOLOMON ET AL (168) AND GLYNN (67).

HUMAN	V-STUDY	DRUG	V-CAUSE	ARG1	V-PHYS	ARG2	CONJ
K AND A (99) S ET AL (168) AND G (67)	HAVE MADE MORE DETAILED STUDIES OF	{CARDIAC {GLYCOSIDES	AFFECT	SODIUM	MOVE IN	RED CELLS	AND
				POTASSIUM	[MOVE IN]	[RED CELLS]	.

FIGURE 3

nominal form of the verb take up, so it is mapped into the
verb column. A transformation hunts for the arguments of the
verb among the adjuncts of the nominal form (uptake) and maps
them into the verb-argument slots. As illustrated in the
format of this simple sentence, the major fact type in this
pharmacology material was composed of an elementary assertion
drawn from a prior science (cell physiology, biochemistry),
with the pharmacological agent entering only on a higher
grammatical level, as an operator on the elementary assertion.

Fact vs. "Meta-fact"

The somewhat longer sentence formatted in Figure 3 util-
izes format columns that were not shown in Figure 2 because
they were empty there. Notice the two new columns on the
left, labelled HUMAN and V-STUDY. Factual assertions involving only the concrete objects of investigation in the science and their interrelations (the two inner sections of the
format) are syntactically separable by the computer from the
words describing the scientists relation to the facts. Verbs
like study, present, discuss, assume, report, which have ex-
clusively human subject nouns and carry the connotation of
the scientists' intellectual activity appear as higher level
operators on the operator-structure already built up from
the words in the "object language" of the science.

Notice also in Figure 3 that there is a conjunction
column CONJ on the right which contains words that connect
one line (or several grouped lines) of the format to another
line or lines. This is a major departure from tables for
quantitative data. Here the conjunction is and, but in other
cases the conjunction may have the form of a verb or a phrase
(e.g. is associated with, is the basis for). Apart from
grammatical conjunctions,only words which have the syntactic
property of operating on a pair of (nominalized) sentences
are accepted in the CONJ column. The words in the CONJ column are much the same in different subfields, whereas the
words in the innermost columns are highly specific to the
field.

A last point to notice in Figure 3 is the presence of
reconstructed word occurrences, shown in square brackets.
The conjunction and is responsible for ellipsis in this case.
Sodium and potassium movements in red cells can be expanded
to sodium movements in red cells and potassium movements in
red cells on the basis of general grammatical properties of
the conjunction and. The expansion of the phrase into two
assertions does not imply that the events are independent of
each other; only that the connection between them is not more
explicit here than their conjoining by and.

LA 721 1.1.5 THE POSSIBILITY THAT ADMINISTRATION OF DIGITALIS, THROUGH ITS INHIBITION OF THE
NA+ - K+ COUPLED SYSTEM, PRODUCES AN INCREASE IN NA+ - CA++ COUPLED TRANSPORT
AND THEREBY AN INCREASE OF INFLUX OF CA++ TO THE MYOFILAMENTS IS DISCUSSED
AND IS PRESENTED AS A POSSIBLE BASIS FOR THE MECHANISM OF DIGITALIS ACTION.

HUMAN	V-STUDY	DRUG	V-CAUSE	V-QUANT	ARG1	V-PHYS	ARG2	CONJ
[AUTHOR]	DISCUSSES {{ }} 1 2	DIGITALIS (ADMINISTRATION OF)	PRODUCES POSSIBLY	INCREASE	NA+ - CA++ COUPLED	TRANSPORT		AND THEREBY
		[DIGITALIS (ADMINISTRATION OF)]	[PRODUCES]	INCREASE	CA++	INFLUX TO MYOFILAMENTS }2		THROUGH
		[DIGITALIS] ITS	= INHIBITION		NA+ - K+ COUPLED SYSTEM			}1 AND
			{ } 1 1					AS BASIS FOR (POSSIBLE)
[AUTHOR]	PRESENTS	DIGITALIS	ACTION MECHANISM					

FIGURE 4

Data Structures vs. Argument

A third formatted sentence, shown in Figure 4, is sufficiently complex so that it illustrates in itself some of the regularizing effect that formatting achieves for a whole text. When the sentence is read without reference to the format, it is not at all apparent that there is so much repetition of similar elements. As the format shows, the sentence consists of 4 interconnected factual units of the same basic type. The texture, and the intellectual content, comes from interrelations among similar data structures, in the use of conjunctions at different levels of grouping, in the introduction of qualifying modifiers and higher level operators, and in the use of reference, either explicitly via pronouns or implicitly via ellipsis. These features belong to the argument or reasoning in the text, which can be separated from the factual units mapped into the inner portions of the format lines. Turning first to the individual fact units in Figure 4, the inner portion of the first line, stripped of its qualifiers, says that digitalis produces an increase in $Na^+ - Ca^{++}$ coupled transport. In this unit, $\underline{Na^+ - Ca^{++}\ coupled\ transport}$ is an instance of the formula $N_{ION}\ V_{MOVE}\ N_{CELL}$ seen previously, even though the cell-word is not present here. In oft-repeated material, the subject or object of the verb is frequently dropped, or sometimes the verb if it is unique to the stated subject or object. This is the case in the third line, where transport is suppressed but easily reconstructed because of the subject, $\underline{Na^+ - K^+\ coupled}$ $\underline{system}$.

Notice in Figure 4 the presence of a new column V-QUANT between the innermost assertion and the columns DRUG, V-CAUSE. The V-QUANT column was not shown in preceding figures because no words like increase, decrease, etc. were present in the sentences. In line 3, the V-QUANT column appears to be empty. But in effect the word inhibition covers both the V-CAUSE and V-QUANT columns, since elsewhere we find in similar contexts that inhibit and cause a decrease in are used interchangeably.

The format in Figure 4 introduces the use of pronouns and other devices of reference. In the third line, the antecedent of the pronoun its, namely digitalis, has been reconstructed as the subject of inhibit. This follows the pattern throughout, that the class of pharmacological agents occurs as the subject of verbs in the V-CAUSE class. (Syntactically, in this sentence, the entire phrase administration of digitalis may be the subject of inhibit; but it matters little to the representation of the information in the sentence, since in this sublanguage, digitalis and the administration of digitalis are used interchangeably as

ON THE DAY OF ADMISSION SWELLING WAS NOTED OF THE LEFT TIBIA AND FOOT AND WAS ASSOCIATED WITH TENDERNESS. SHE WAS SEEN THE NIGHT BEFORE ADMISSION IN THE EMERGENCY ROOM BECAUSE OF A TEMPERATURE OF 105, AND NO CAUSE NOTED. THERE WAS NO EVIDENCE OF UPPER RESPIRATORY INFECTION.

		TREATMENT				PATIENT STATE					TIME			
CONJ	PATIENT	INST	V-TREAT	T-P CON	BODY-PART	BODY-MEAS	QUANT	SIGN/SYMPT	EVIDENCE	P	Q	UNIT	P	REF. PT.
1					LEFT TIBIA			SWELLING	WAS NOTED	ON		THE DAY	OF	ADMISSION
2 AND					[LEFT] FOOT			[SWELLING]	[WAS NOTED]	[ON		THE DAY	OF	ADMISSION]
3 AND						1-2								
4 WAS ASSOCIATED WITH								TENDERNESS						
5 .	SHE	EMERGENCY ROOM	WAS SEEN	BECAUSE OF		TEMPERATURE	105					THE NIGHT BE-FORE		ADMISSION
6 .					UPPER RESPIRATORY			INFECTION	THERE WAS NO EVIDENCE					

FIGURE 5

subjects of V-CAUSE verbs.)

The fourth format line has the interesting property
that the whole object language, or factual, portion of the
format is empty of physically occurring words. The three
preceding format lines, seen as a unit, are repeated implicitly as the first operand (subject) of the binary relation
is a basis for, where the second operand (object) is the
mechanism of digitalis action. Reasoning in science writing
is characterized by devices of this sort. A single assertion becomes a nominalized sentence within another sentence;
a sequence of interconnected sentences becomes an element of
a later sentence by implicit repetition or by pronominal reference (this, this process, etc.). In this way it becomes
possible for complicated interrelations to be expressed in
the physically linear medium of language.

PROPERTIES OF SCIENCE INFORMATION

From a study of information formats in different subfields, one gets a picture of how scientific information is
carried by language both in respect to the unique informational characteristics of each science and in respect to the
general properties of information viewed over science as a
whole.

First, the information formats of a particular science
reflect the properties of information in that particular science in contrast with other sciences. The pharmacology formats, for example, displayed a characteristic predicational
hierarchy in which the pharmacological agent occurred on a
higher grammatical level as an operator on an inner sentence
from cell physiology or biochemistry, reflecting the role of
the drug as an outside element that affects on-going processes. Quantity and quantity-change were important in the
pharmacology formats (not all quantity columns are shown in
the example formats, e.g. dosage) reflecting the importance
of quantity relations in this science. This type of format
contrasts with one that was obtained for a corpus of clinical reporting, where both the columns and the relations
among the columns were quite different. An example of the
clinical format is shown in Figure 5 in a simplified version
and without further explanation simply to illustrate a different information structure. In the clinical format, time
columns are essential to the information, whereas they were
almost entirely absent in the pharmacology formats. In the
clinical formats, there is very little predicational hierarchy and virtually no argument, both of which were present
in the pharmacology formats. The structure of the clinical
information, displayed in the formats, is an interplay

between columns containing treatment words and columns containing words that describe the patient's state; successive rows are linked primarily through time sequence, with the conjunction columns playing a secondary role.

While the formats for different subfields differ, as they should, to capture the specific character of information in each field, they have certain properties in common that hold for all of science writing. To mention just a few:

(1) Statements about science facts are separated by the grammar itself from the science facts proper; the role of the human investigator is syntactically separable from the report of factual events.

(2) The report of a complex event has a structure composed of a hierarchy of different types of operators, the ultimate "bottom level" operand being the carrier of the most elementary objects and events. When a given science draws upon a prior science, the material from the prior science appears as the operand of material from the given science.

(3) Argument is carried by connectives between the data structures built up in this hierarchical fashion. Whole units are carried forward by the telescoping of an operator-hierarchy into a single noun phrase or a substitute "pro-word," or by the controlled dropping of words permitted by the grammar.

(4) What is universal is the amount of repetition and regularity that is found in all science writing, once stylistic variations and equivalent grammatical forms are eliminated. Every individual piece of writing contains some repetition (or it would not be connected discourse). Across a single specialized discipline, the same items repeat in different combinations and with variations, as though all the texts were part of a single extended discourse. Although the texts each bring in some new feature they are sufficiently similar as to fit into an overall formulaic characterization. These formulas, or information formats, are then a powerful tool for organizing information on a given topic, when that information comes from diverse sources and in diverse forms.

The common features in information formats, noted in (1)-(4) above, suggest that a generalized matrix for all factual writing in science is a possibility. Such a matrix could provide guidelines for the development of new types of data structures in computerized information systems, which in the future should be able to handle information from the natural language part of texts as well as citation information, numerical data, and other forms of information. At present, it appears that this matrix could be tabular in form (a numerical table would

be a special case), but should allow for more than two dimensions, and in particular would have the following special features:

(a)   Columns or groups of columns could be specified to have
      a hierarchical operator-operand relation between them
      (expressing levels of predication if present).

(b)   A distinguished column or columns would carry connectives
      between successive rows or groups of rows (expressing
      conjunction in language).

(c)   Provision would be made for pointers from an element in
      one row to an element of another row, or to an entire row
      or group of rows (accommodating pronouns and other refer-
      entials).

Even at this early stage of work on a generalized matrix,
we have some information with regard to the types of columns
that can be expected, for example, EVENT, QUANTITY, TIME,
CONDITION, CONNECTIVE, though not every science will have all
of these. The EVENT columns will always be present; every
science has some elementary assertions concerning the primary
objects of investigation. While the content of the sub columns of an EVENT unit varies from science to science, the existence of "bottom level" elements and relations is universal.

In view of the importance of quantitative data in many
sciences, columns for QUANTITY and QUANTITY-CHANGE will undoubtedly often be needed. Fortunately, quantity words have
distinctive linguistic properties which enable them to be
recognized by the computer and treated specially. The same
holds true for time words and the mapping of time words into
TIME columns.

Many factual statements in science contain a statement of
the conditions under which the statement applies or under
which the reported observation was made. These conditions
usually occur syntactically as adverbial modifiers, and hence
can be sent into CONDITION columns, even if the content is not
repetitive enough to have special columns for it in the matrix.
It will be extremely interesting to see how the selection of
specific columns varies from field to field as the matrix is
further tested.

The CONNECTIVE column is universal. Through it are
channeled the links between individual facts, which links are
important both for retrieval and for further characterization
of the information content. A wealth of data about scientific
information lies in the contents of the CONNECTIVE column.
The procedures we have developed isolate the factual units and
align them. What is left, if it is not "meta-fact" (the
scientist's own relation to the facts that goes into its own

columns) is connective material. The connectives are not
just grammatical conjunctions, but also verbs and other expressions which carry causal and other relations. A study
of this material would yield a great deal of practical in-
sight into the "grammar of science." Since we know that on
the one hand the connectives of logic are not sufficient to
carry scientific reasoning and on the other hand the full
power of natural language is too rich, we could home in, by
empirical study, on just what types of connectives are used,
and possibly develop sets of synonym classes which would represent the basic connectives in most frequent use. Such a
result would have wide implications both for practical information processing and for the philosophy of science.

COMPUTER PROGRAMS

A battery of computer programs have been developed to
do the language analysis and information formatting described
above. The basic tool, without which the long, complicated
sentences of scientific writing could not be machine-analyzed,
is a large computerized grammar of English (2). This grammar, which required a reorganization of language data into
a computable system, was developed over a period of years
with support from the National Science Foundation. The grammar is applied to sentences by a parsing program which has
gone through several implemented versions (3, 4). The lat-
est version (5) runs on the CDC 6600, and includes a special
programming language (6) and its compiler as part of the system, as well as a component for executing transformational
procedures (7). Among the implemented transformations, one
worthy of special note because it overcomes a special complexity of language is the procedure for expanding conjunc-
tional sequences to their full explicit form (8).

Mention has been made of the fact that the sublanguage
word classes are defined on distributional rather than semantic grounds. A clustering program (9) was written to do just
that: to calculate similarity coefficients for all word
pairs based on the frequency with which they both occurred
in the same grammatical relation to the same other words, and
to form classes of those words whose calculated similarity
coefficients were higher than a given threshold. Details of
this algorithm are given in the paper cited. It was found
that the word classes formed in this way correlated well with
classes that had been defined semantically for the same material.

The information formats for a given subfield are developed by people, not by machine, even though a number of the
components for doing the job are at hand: the programs for

sentence analysis and transformation, and the program for
sublanguage word-class generation. Nevertheless, it is a
task of some complexity to abstract the major patterns or
formulas of subfield information.

The major use of the computer programs thus far is in
subfield applications. Once the information format is clearly
specified and the word classes are defined, formatting transformations are written which map the output of the parsing
and regularizing programs into the columns of the implemented format. To date, we have had the opportunity of carrying out the complete process on a sample of English-language
radiology reports (1, 10) and currently on clinical records
(hospital discharge summaries). In principle, and I believe
in practice, the methods should apply in any subfield where
the subject matter is relatively circumscribed and words are
used in a relatively constant way. An initial "tooling up"
is of course required for each subfield application, in
order to develop the specific formats and subfield word dictionary required by the formatting programs.

In addition, it should be stressed that each subfield
application is not a programming task that begins afresh.
On the contrary, both the computer tools and the type of information structures produced are quite general. With regard
to tools, it must be clear that if the grammar of English
used by the computer did not have a broad coverage of the
language, it would not be possible for the system to analyze
sentences from many different kinds of texts, which it has
been shown able to do. In addition, a large amount of grammatical detail is required in order to obtain the correct
parse (or a small number of parses if the sentence is actually ambiguous). The computer grammar scores high in this regard; in applications, our experience has been that the first
parse formats correctly in over 85% of the sentences.

With regard to information structures, the general matrix for science writing described above provides the framework for the implementations of formats for specific subfields. Each application is approached as a problem in
tailoring the general programs for use on a particular subject matter. Also, particular features that repeat are generalized. The implemented framework approaches more and more
a general program for formatting the information in scientific documents.

FUTURE INFORMATION SYSTEMS

Computer programs for processing natural language are
reaching the stage of application at a time when changes in

the technology of information production and dissemination
are making computerized natural language data bases widely
available. In addition to the well-established library-
oriented data bases, there are now many large special-purpose
computer stores in the form of files and records, whose mag-
nitude is such that there is a need for computer programs to
access and summarize the different kinds of information in
the documents. In this setting, a computer capability for
processing natural language takes on practical importance.

The fact that large computerized stores of information
in natural language form are being created in publishing and
in record-keeping is in itself creating a demand for techniques which can process data in natural language form. This
is true not only in the area of official scientific publication, where a change in printing technology makes such data
bases possible, but also in the area of file management,
where institutions in medicine, industry, and government find
it convenient to put large stores of natural language records
into computer-readable form, primarily for convenience of
access and storage, but also, hopefully, to do retrieval and
routine processing automatically.

An example of this process on a small scale in an insti-
tutional framework is the case of a hospital which computer-
izes its patient files for quick back-up to the written
charts and for transactional purposes; then, finding itself
with this large natural language data base, seeks computer
techniques for processing the contents of the documents to
obtain the summaries and other information required for
health care evaluation. We are bound to see a pressure of
this sort arising wherever natural language files are computerized. Once information is available in computer readable form, users inevitably want the computer to process it.

Viewing the future of information services broadly,
F.W. Lancaster recently made these projections (11):

The pattern is more or less inevitable: more
data bases in natural language form because "publication" itself will be electronic; more searching of
data bases directly by scientists because these files
will be readily accessible through terminals in of-
fices and homes; more need for a natural language
search approach because the person who is not an
information specialist will not want to learn the
idiosyncracies of a conventional controlled vocabulary and, even if he were willing to master one
controlled vocabulary, the range of data bases that
will be readily accessible to him virtually precludes

the conventional controlled vocabulary approach.

Those concerned with the design of information systems should now be concentrating on functional requirements for the user-oriented, natural language systems of the future.

There are several different ways in which natural language processing techniques may contribute to information systems in the future. For one, natural language might be the preferred medium of communication of the user with the system, as suggested by the above quotation and by others in the information field (12). When the techniques of dialogue analysis and interpretation are further advanced, programs should be able to sort requests according to the type of response which would be appropriate and guide the user to find the desired information in the computer store. Successful experiments with this type of system have been made (13). Such programs could serve as a front end to existing document retrieval systems as well as to systems which include other information services.

Natural language processing techniques could also be important in locating and retrieving specific information, i.e. in "fact retrieval." In testing whether particular documents, or parts of documents, in the data base contained the information requested, advanced techniques such as formatting might be applied to both the document and the request. This would test whether there was a match of fact pattern, as opposed to just an overlap in vocabulary. To obtain the proper passages to test in this way, the technique of answer-passage retrieval (14) might be appropriate.

In restricted subject areas, an extension of some of the more sophisticated programs being developed could perform some of the data processing tasks now performed by research and clerical assistants, e.g. sorting, filing, retrieving, screening and summarizing information in natural language from various source documents, according to given categories. These functions are, of course, a tall order for computers. However, the basis for such programs is being laid in the work described in this paper and in (15). This research, in conjunction with other basic studies in information science such as those reported in this symposium, are looking ahead to a future information technology which combines advances in computer capabilities with knowledge about the nature of information, to solve the problem of the information explosion. A new information technology could turn what is now a burden--too much accumulated information--into a resource, by providing scientists and technologists with direct access,

via user-oriented computer systems, to the large and increasing stores of knowledge.

ACKNOWLEDGEMENTS

The research reported in this paper was supported in
part by the National Science Foundation under grant no.
SIS 75-22945 of the Division of Science Information, and in
part by research grant 1-R01-LM-02616 from the National
Library of Medicine, National Institutes of Health, DHEW.

REFERENCES

1. Hirschman, L., and R. Grishman, Fact Retrieval from
    Natural Language Medical Records. Submitted for publi-
    cation in Medinfo 1977.
2. Sager, N., A Computer String Grammar of English. String
    Program Reports (S.P.R.) No. 4, Linguistic String Pro-
    ject, New York University, 1968.
3. Raze, C., The FAP Program for String Decomposition of
    Scientific Texts. S.P.R. No. 2, Linguistic String Pro-
    ject, New York University, 1967.
4. Grishman, R., The Implementation of the String Parser of
    English. In Natural Language Processing, R. Rustin, ed.,
    Algorithmics Press, New York, 1973.
5. Grishman, R., N. Sager, C. Raze, and B. Bookchin, The
    Linguistic String Parser. Proceedings of the 1973 Com-
    puter Conference, 427-434, AFIPS Press, Montvale, N.J.
    1973.
6. Sager, N. and R. Grishman, The Restriction Language for
    Computer Grammars of Natural Language. Communications
    of the ACM, vol. 18, 390-400, 1975.
7. Hobbs, J. and R. Grishman, The Automatic Transformational
    Analysis of English Sentences: An Implementation.
    International Journal of Computer Mathematics, in press.
8. Raze, C., The Parsing and Transformational Expansion of
    Coordinate Conjunction Strings. S.P.R. No. 11, Linguis-
    tic String Project, New York University, 1976.
9. Hirschman, L., R. Grishman and N. Sager, Grammatically-
    based Automatic Word Class Formation. Information Pro-
    cessing and Management, vol. 11, 39-57, 1975.
10. Hirschman, L., Grishman, R., Sager, N., From Text to
    Structured Information: Automatic Processing of Medical
    Reports, Proceedings of the 1976 National Computer Con-
    ference, AFIPS Press, Montvale, N.J., 1976.
11. Lancaster, F.W. The Relevance of Linguistics to Informa-
    tion, Proceedings of the 1976 FID/LD Workshop on Lin-
    guistics and Information Science, in press.
12. Panel: Can Present Methods for Library and Information
    Retrieval Service Survive?, Proceedings of the 1971

Annual Conference of the ACM, 564-567.

13. Hillman, Donald J., Customized User Services Via Interactions with LEADERMART, Information Storage and Retrieval 9, 587-596, 1973.

14. O'Connor, John, Retrieval of Answer-Sentences and Answer
Figures from Papers by Text-Searching, Information Processing and Management, 11, 155-164, 1975.

15. Sager, N., Evaluation of Automated Natural Language Processing in the Further Development of Science Information Retrieval, Final Report to the Division of Science
Information of the National Science Foundation; S.P.R.
No. 10, Linguistic String Project, New York University,
1976.

4

Knowledge Transfer Systems

Donald J. Hillman

1. The Evolving Knowledge Society

There is much contemporary interest in the notion of a "post-industrial" society, that is, a society which no longer places most of its emphasis on industrial production. What may be considered to have replaced that emphasis depends very much on individual points of view, prejudices, and, in some cases, polemics. The debate, however, is premature, since the shape of things to come is still too indefinite to permit confident forecasts. Nevertheless, there has been a definite shift in Western society from industrial production to service activities during the last twenty-five years or so, sufficient to stimulate conjecture as to the final form of the transition.

To a large extent, the shift has been governed by advances in computers and communications ("the second industrial revolution"). To these generally smooth movements we must add recent events and conditions of a more disruptive nature, such as the recurring energy crisis. This is hardly deserving of the name "crisis", since the amount of available energy has not suddenly diminished. Yet, on an international scale, the set of events labeled "the energy crisis" has had the apparent effect of reducing the amount of available energy, although the real causes are selective withholding of energy, price increases, and accelerated energy consumption. What the crisis and the severe current winter have been very effective in doing is to make perfectly clear that the supply of energy is not unlimited, and this realization has

profoundly altered our thinking. Because we cannot
make economic plans on the assumption of unlimited
supplies of energy and materials, we must consider
placing limits on our physical growth. These
problems, together with our concerns over environmental pollution, unrestrained population growth,
and inadequate food supplies for much of the less
developed world, have challenged and continue to
challenge the institutions and procedures that were
set up to foster and manage the growth of industrial production.

Moreover, the challenge is a complex one,
since our way of life is not only threatened by
global problems, but is also being far more subtly
transformed by the redistribution of the work
force from production and manufacturing employment
into information-handling activities. A recent
estimate (1) states that some 50% of the United
States labor force is involved in the information
sector, accounting for 30% of the Gross National
Product. As observed earlier, this shift has been
heavily influenced by the truly remarkable advances
made in computers and communications technology. It
is not only the volume of material that can be
processed by computer/communication systems but
also the rapidly increasing variety of applications
that make the changes to our way of life so swift
and so pervasive. From relatively simple word-
processing systems to more sophisticated (and more
significant) electronic funds transfer systems,
the trend is definitely towards a "paperless
society". The challenge is thus to know how to use
the newly emerged and still developing computer/
communications technology in coping with problems
which have been with us for a long time but have
recently become prominent or have been suddenly
aggravated by world conditions.

There are different responses to this challenge, which are examined below. The aim of this
paper is not to argue in favor of any one of these,
but to address the fundamental problem of building
a sound theoretical structure for any worthwhile
response. As the title indicates, the most promising type of response will be in terms of knowledge transfer as opposed to more conventional kinds
of information handling. The theme of this paper
is thus that the emergence of a society in which

information processing occupies more of the work
force than industrial production is only the first
stage of an evolutionary process, whose later
stages will feature a constantly increasing emphasis on the way in which information can be system-
atized and organized. It is this feature, of
course, that distinguishes knowledge from information, and it forms the basis of the discussion that
follows.

2. Knowledge Versus Information

We have yet to establish our claim that
computers will be used to transfer knowledge as
opposed to information in the society we contem-
plate, and that the manipulation and application
of knowledge to societal problems will emerge as a
distinctive activity in that society. It is not
difficult, however, to build such a scenario.
Successively more powerful and useful data structures have been devised and put to use in data
processing technology over the last several years,
and it is easy to imagine how those structures
could form the basis for other formalisms that permit ever greater varieties of logical operations.
Specifically, it is possible to envisage a set of
structures and functions that constitute a model of
knowledge transfer. In order to do this, we must
first distinguish between knowledge and information, and then use this distinction to show how
computers can bring knowledge to bear on societal
problems.

It is undoubtedly the case that knowledge
consists of organized bodies of information. However, a card catalog is an organized body of
information, but it would hardly qualify as knowledge. The question then becomes what kind of
organization is characteristic of knowledge.

A notable feature of much information acquired
in the course of ordinary experience is that, although the information may be accurate enough
within certain limits, it is seldom accompanied by
any explanation of why the facts are as they are
perceived to be. By contrast, it is the desire for
explanations that generates knowledge, and it is
the organization and classification of knowledge on
the basis of explanatory principles that is the

distinctive goal of science. More particularly,
scientific knowledge seeks to discover and to
formulate in general terms the conditions under
which events of various kinds occur. The statements of these determining conditions then function
as explanations of the corresponding happenings.

Now knowledge in the sense of scientific
knowledge can be achieved by distinguishing or
isolating certain properties in the subject matter
in question and by ascertaining the repeatable
patterns of dependence in which these properties
are related to each other. In highly developed
sciences, such as physics, patterns of relations
are discovered that apply to vast ranges of facts,
so that with the help of a small number of explanatory principles an indefinitely large number of
assertions about these facts can be shown to
constitute a logically unified body of knowledge.
Newton's Principia is an outstanding example of a
hypothetico-deductive system in which a few principles show that assertions concerning planetary
motion, the behavior of the tides, the paths of
projectiles, and the rise of liquids in thin tubes
are intimately related, and that all these assertions can be rigorously deduced from those principles in conjunction with various special factual
assumptions.

Of course, not all of the bodies of organized
knowledge that we deal with exhibit the highly
integrated form of systematic explanation which
Newtonian mechanics displays. Nor is it likely
that the knowledge transfer systems we are capable
of developing will come anywhere near Newtonian
mechanics in either deductive rigor or explanatory
fertility. Rather, the type of knowledge that our
systems will be able to handle and transfer is
much more likely to be technoscientific or problem-
solving knowledge. Chiaraviglio and Gehl (2) have
conceputalized knowledge in terms of a spectrum
that extends from technoscience at one extreme to
hypothetico-deductive schemes at the other, and
stipulate that different types of knowledges can be
arrayed along the spectrum in terms of how they
were generated and how they are warranted. The
latter notion is explained as follows:

"Technoscientific knowledge is warranted
by its results. It is "successful" insofar
as it leads to problem solution; otherwise,
it "fails." Values from the success-
failure axis are immediately applicable to
problem solving plans and derivately to the
knowledge on which the plans are based. In
contrast, scientific knowledge is warranted
by evidence. Thus values from the truth-
falsity axis are applicable to hypotheses
based on evidence. Of course, there are
connections between the success-failure and
truth-falsity axes, but these connections
are not simple and they may well depend on
how relevant knowledges were generated."(3)

Problem-solving knowledge, according to this
explanation, is generated first in the form of a
problem statement describing a problem situation.
A problem solution will then consist of a plan
which, when properly executed, will yield a solution to the problem as stated. This analysis of
problem-solving knowledge and its application
corresponds very well with a view of information
science as a body of prescriptive rules, and it is
worth taking the time to examine this position
before proceeding any further.

The major issue addressed in this symposium is
that of strengthening the theoretical structure of
information science. This problem has proved to be
strangely elusive during the admittedly brief
period since information science began to emerge in
some recognizable form. In its simplest terms, the
problem is that the theory of information science
has always lagged behind its practice. This has
given rise to the misconception that the theory
should attempt to provide an explanation for some
observed set of phenomena, in this case the observable aspects of retrieval situations. Hence
the misguided attempts to set up information
science in terms of a descriptive or explanatory
scheme. Nothing, however, stands in need of
explanation outside of certain kinds of distributional phenomena, which have satisfactory statistical descriptions (e.g. Bradford's Law). A far
more profitable approach to information science is
to identify a body of principles or rules which can
be applied in a prescriptive sense to achieve a
desired outcome. It is this interpretation of

information science that lends itself so completely
to the idea of delivering problem-solving knowledge
in response to societal needs, and I shall adopt
this prescriptive interpretation in developing a
theoretical structure for the transfer of technoscientific knowledge.

3. A Knowledge Transfer Model

We now have a good enough distinction between
knowledge and information to allow us to address
the question how computers can be used to transfer
knowledge rather than information. Clearly, the
answer will be in terms of recurrent patterns of
dependence in which factual data and certain of
their properties stand to one another. Recognition
of those patterns and the identification of repeatable structures in bodies of information will
then form the basis for organizing retrieved data
into assemblages that resemble individual pieces
of knowledge. In some instances the assemblages
will provide knowledge that something is the case,
or that various events or activities are related in
certain ways. In other instances, the assemblages
will provide knowledge how to do something, or
what procedures to follow in seeking a desired outcome or determinate result. In any event, the
assemblages will do much more than provide individual bits of information, whether bibliographic or
otherwise.

Our first step in constructing a theoretical
structure for knowledge transfer is to formulate
an abstract model. The approach* we shall follow
is to model a computer-aided knowledge transfer
system as an integrated and codified structure of
logically and conceptually related components in
which characteristic kinds of "knowledge flow" (in
senses to be determined) are controlled, monitored,
and promoted by man-machine interactions. Such a
model presumes the availability of a resource-
sharing computer-communications network as the
domain of knowledge transfer, so that the implications of networking for knowledge transfer become
an important secondary concern.

---

*This approach is based on research supported by
the National Science Foundation under Grant No.
SIS75-09282.

One virtue of our model is that it enables us to represent the development of a knowledge transfer system as a process of progressive conceptual enhancement of interactive information transfer systems in a resource-sharing network. This is a very practical advantage, in that we can study and simulate the effects of increasing and refining the truly knowledge-related aspects of a system by enhancing its information transfer capabilities. In this way, we can characterize knowledge transfer in terms of a continuum of information transfer activities, permitting successive approximations to a knowledge transfer system as those information transfer activities become more intimately related and organized on the strength of repeatable patterns of dependence. Another advantage is that we can treat knowledge as being generable and deliverable <u>via</u> networks of information processing facilities <u>and</u> algorithms essentially of the kind we now possess. This will go a long way toward preserving continuity between information transfer and knowledge transfer system development.

The distinguishing aspect of any system, whether of the knowledge transfer or information transfer variety, is the interaction among its various components. We have suggested that enhancing the interactions between various nodes of an information transfer network provides a means for approximating knowledge transfer. Whatever model we choose to represent knowledge transfer must therefore depict various kinds of "knowledge flow" between network components, and be capable of showing how each kind of flow can be controlled, monitored, and promoted by man-machine interactions. A <u>flowgraph</u> model suggests itself naturally for this purpose, in which different kinds of knowledge users, different kinds of transfer nodes, and different kinds of knowledge can be represented.

The model we opt for contains two types of nodes, <u>viz.</u>, distributive and contributive nodes. A distributive node is one at which at most one information flow terminates and at least two originate. This is shown as node D in Fig. 1.

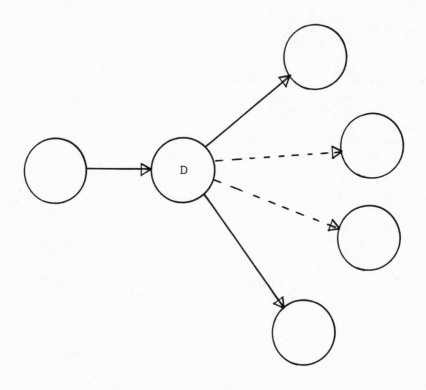

Fig. 1.   Distributive Node

A contributive node is one at which at least
two information flows terminate and at most one
originates. This is shown as node C in Fig. 2.

The virtue of these simple concepts is that
they permit us to represent "knowledge flow" in
terms of concentrations of information flows
terminating at a given node A and issuing as a
single flow directed at another node B. Node B in
turn may reissue the unified knowledge flow as a
set of reorganized or decomposed flows representing different knowledge transmittances, such as
specific "how to" prescriptions conforming to
given initial or boundary conditions. For example,
node A in Fig. 3 could act as the concentrator of
information flows concerning the extracted volume
and characteristics of bituminous coals from deep
mines, strip mines, Auger mines, and refuse mines,
all located in a given geographical location.
Within node A, these separate information flows
are examined for recurrent structural features or
dependencies. This, of course, entails that the
flows are repeated over time. If it is possible
to isolate certain properties of the data being
transmitted in the flows of information, and to
ascertain repeatable patterns in which these
properties are related to one another, then it
might be possible for node A to contribute a
solitary knowledge flow that indicates, for
example, the total BTU content of coal energy as
a result of refining operations.

This single knowledge flow could in turn terminate at node B, and be distributed as specialized knowledge flows concerning the transportation
of coal-derived energy forms by rail, truck,river,
and tidewater. Node C might then act as another
concentrator of transportation knowledge flows,
and contribute an integrated knowledge flow pertaining to the planned or allocated end use of
coal-derived energy that is to be transported by,
say, rail and truck to electrical utilities in a
given region over a stipulated period of time.
Here, the ability of node C to concentrate knowledge flows would presumably rest on whatever
repeatable dependencies could be established among
consumption data, weather conditions, demand
factors, vehicle availabilities, etc. for the
place-time complex involved. Fig. 3 depicts the

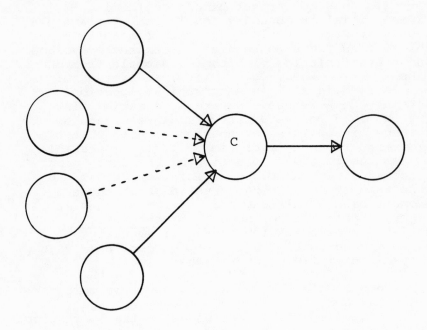

Fig. 2 <u>Contributive Node</u>

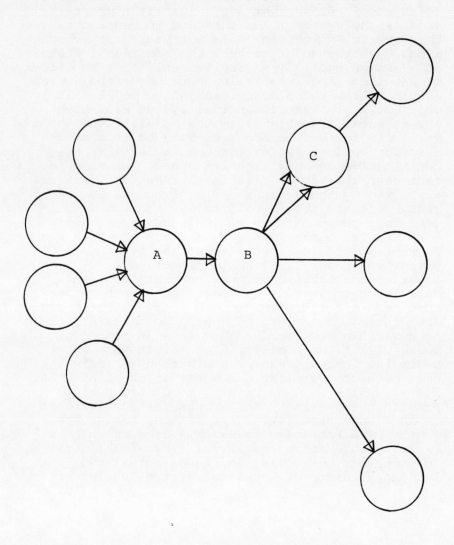

Fig. 3   Knowledge Flow Network

situation just described.

The knowledge transfer model described above
is an iconic flowgraph, i.e., its structure re-
sembles the system it is intended to represent.
That system, of course, does not yet exist, which
means that the model assumes the additional status
of a design tool. This implies only that the flows
of knowledge and information throughout the system
should follow those described in the model. It
does not imply that the actual system will have
any physical resemblance to the model, although if
we are to follow the model we must be able to
describe various system components in terms of
contributive and distributive nodes. We have in
fact been able to do this in the research program
supported by the National Science Foundation already referred to. Specifically, we have identified four components to be included in the design
of a knowledge transfer system, each of which can
be represented in terms of contributive and distributive nodes. They are, respectively, a
question-analyzer, an answer determination and
delivery component, a database management component, and a collection of data sets. Since these
are crucial components of knowledge transfer, it
is desirable to describe them in some detail,
which will be done below. Each of these components is, in one sense or another, a logical
outgrowth of a similar component in the LEADERMART
System, which will be briefly described next to
provide the necessary background for our research
in knowledge transfer. In addition, basing the
design of a knowledge transfer system on an
existing information retrieval system will serve
to underline our belief in the essential evolutionary nature of knowledge system development.

3.1   The LEADERMART System

During the late nineteen-sixties and early
nineteen-seventies, the National Science Foundation
supported the development of six university information systems. The LEADERMART System of Lehigh
University was one of these, and provided a user-
oriented operational information retrieval facility,
called LEADER (LEhigh Automatic Device for Efficient Retrieval), within the framework of the Mart
Science and Engineering Library. Three major
classes of users were involved, viz. scientists
and engineers associated with interdisciplinary research centers at Lehigh University; agencies of
the federal government, such as the Environmental
Protection Agency, and the National Bureau of Standards; and industrial users.

The data bases for the service represented a
blend of general coverage and special purpose requirements. The Lehigh Center for Information
Science was licensed by the Chemical Abstracts
Service as one of its Information Centers, with
Condensates as the primary data base. A similar
licensing arrangement with Engineering Index, Inc.,
provided the Center with COMPENDEX. A third general data base was the Library of Congress MARC II
file, which formed the basis of Lehigh's on-line
library cataloging system and the core of its
library automation project.

These three general purpose data bases func-
tioned as "wholesale" components of LEADERMART. A
special purpose data base, constructed and maintained at Lehigh, acts as a "retail" product.
This is the file on Tall Buildings,created for a
project of the same name run by the International
Association of Bridge and Structural Engineers and
the American Society of Civil Engineers.

A major difference between LEADERMART and
other operational systems was that it was conceived, designed, and implemented as an on-line,
interactive system from the very beginning. Its
off-line, batch features are background activities,
and can be used in a secondary role in so far as
information retrieval is concerned. The primary
retrieval activity within LEADERMART took the form
of a dialogue between a user and a system, whose

objective was to reach a joint decision as to the
nature, volume, pertinence, and utility of the
information to be retrieved, displayed and manipulated.

In order to provide the conditions for such a
dialogue, a very considerable software development
program was carried out between 1965 and 1971.
During this time, the complete LEADERMART software
was written, tested, refined, and implemented over
four successive hardware configurations, culminating in a CDC6400.

Text-processing software is extensive. For
example, full text entry can be handled by LETEXT,
which is a data-editing, non-numeric, non-inter-
pretive compiler providing extensive on-line
editing and error correction features. These
features proved to be invaluable assets for clean-
ing up input errors in high volume data files.
Each input document, whether full text or abstract,
was analyzed on a sentence-by-sentence basis for
automatic indexing and characterization. The
software for these purposes is entirely unique to
LEADERMART. A string-processing language called
SMILES (String Manipulation Interpretive Language
for Easy Syntax) was written for the CDC6400, preceded by similar languages (LECOM I,II and III)
for a GE 225 and an IBM 1800. This language provided the vehicle for the LEGRAM analysis procedure, which can perform logico-syntactic analysis of input sentences to reduce them to their
underlying logical relations. Once the logical
form of a sentence has been identified, it is
possible to pick out its topic-denoting expressions and to determine how they are related to
each other as arguments of n-termed predicates.
This permits not only the automatic selection of
index terms but also the creation of logical
connections between such terms for loading into
the file generation subsystem.

The files provide, among other things, a complete record of every conceptual liaison between
index terms, permitting a retrieval dialogue in
which users are presented with topics logically
related to those specified in their input requests.
The requests themselves are usually presented via
CRT to LEADERMART in the form of English sentences, with no restrictions on vocabulary. It

proved to be far more efficient to have users describe their interests in their own prose narrative terms than to impose the constraints of artificial forms. By conducting a highly interactive dialogue with the system, the user can fine-tune his inquiry on the basis of conceptual matches and selective responses. He can narrow or broaden his search at will, or quickly terminate one unprofitable direction and choose another. The retrieval process can be entered and re-entered at any point, or suspended and reactivated. Each prior search of a user is remembered and stored as a dynamic "profile" to be executed if desired on subsequent occasions or against updated data bases.

The user is presented with information judged by LEADERMART to be pertinent to his inquiry. Such information is displayed and ranked on the basis of decreasing pertinence, where "pertinence" is a structural notion. He may select or reject such pertinent items on the basis of acceptability, which is a behavioral notion peculiar to each user. In this way, the LEADERMART system was able to accommodate the preferences and idiosyncracies of all its users, whose behavior patterns showed substantial variations.

3.2   Question-Analyzer

This component of our knowledge transfer design shows the clearest lineal descent from the text-processing software of LEADERMART. The LEADERMART front-end was, of course, capable of carrying out a dialogue with users, and our objective here was to extend this capability into the realm of question-answering. This took the practical form of being able to determine interactively what the presuppositions of a user's question were, and what kind of answer he was looking for. A new front-end, QUANSY, was designed for this purpose,and includes the following features:

a) a dynamic search-formulation technique;
b) a "manipulative" interface;
                      and
c) a mechanism for interfacing day-to-day
   information with database information.

The most important job for QUANSY is to answer questions. This it does by first translating questions into their corresponding declarative forms, and then treating them in terms of the operations to be performed on input text, i.e. factual assertions about some subject matter of interest to users, e.g. coal production. This subject matter is very appropriate for the study of problem-solving knowledge, and was used extensively in the research program being described here.

Each assertion is processed for content, and its content-indicating terms are stripped out and inserted in a dictionary file. The assertion is then syntactically analyzed and converted to a formal structure. Substantival constituents from each structure are inserted into a phrase file, and verb phrases are inserted into a relation file. The process of analysis and file construction is termed "memory construction" in QUANSY, and provides the basis for simple question-answering procedures. The complete cycle is described below.

3.2.1 Memory Structure of QUANSY

There are three substructures in the memory, viz., the term file, the phrase file, and the relation file.

3.2.1.1 Term (Dictionary) File

Each record in this file consists of the following elementary data items:

1. word as a sequence of characters;
2. word code;
3. noun use pointer;
4. adjective use pointer;
5. adverb use pointer;
6. use with non-verb termination pointer;
7. other usages pointer;
8. active generic anchor location in relation file (optional);
9. infinitive usage pointer (optional);
10. present participle usage pointer (optional);
11. past participle usage pointer (optional);
12. unique number;

13. number of characters in word;
                    and
14. verb or non-verb.

The word is kept in its full character representation, regardless of the number of characters
it contains. The word code is a six-digit code
for major syntactic category and subsidiary information. The various pointers indicate uses in the
phrase file unless otherwise noted. The optional
data items 8-11 pertain only to verbs.

The file is alphabetic, and all searches are
binary. To facilitate two-directional access to
the file (without redundant binary searches) a tag
file is maintained according to unique number and
location information. This is particularly important for the create routine described below.

3.2.1.2 Phrase File

This file contains every different phrase
occurring in input sentences. Each record in the
file contains the following data items:

1. a phrase as a sequence of words;
2. pointer to subject usage;
3. pointer to direct object usage;
4. pointer to indirect object usage;
5. pointer to "where?" question-answering
     usage;
6. pointer to "when?" question-answering
7. pointer to "why?" question answering

8. pointer to "what?" question-answering
        usage;
9. pointer to "how?" question-answering
        usage;
10. numerical data in phrase;
11. code for quantifiers in phrase;
12. unique number of last word in phrase;
13. phrase type code

At present, up to 40 characters are stored
for each phrase. This can be expanded as necessary. The eight different pointers for each
phrase identify separate blocks of storage in the
Relation File containing records of grammatical
and question-answering usage for the phrase in
question. Thus the phrase "volumetrically

important coal seam" could be linked by pointers
to several nodes in the Relation File insofar as
assertions are made in the input text concerning
the location, age, productive capacity, reserve
estimates, coal washability, etc. of such seams.

The numerical data and quantifiers in each
phrase are stored separately.

3.2.1.3 Relation File

This file contains all the verb-phrases
occurring in input sentences. Verbs are the most
common vehicles for logical relationships, and
are used in QUANSY to establish such relationships among noun-phrase arguments.

Each record in the Relation File contains the
following data items:

1. a verb anchor;
2. pointers to all occurrences of a single
     grammatical variant of the verb but
     with different qualifiers;
3. each qualifier and its type;
4. pointers to all occurrences of different
     grammatical variants of the verb;
5. type of grammatical variant;
6. arguments of the verb.

A verb anchor is the infinitive of the verb
(without "to"). Examples of a single grammatical
variant of a verb with different qualifiers are
"produced", "slowly produced", "never produced",
etc. Different grammatical variants of the
anchor verb "produce" are e.g. "produces", "has
been produced", "should produce", etc. i.e. those
forms arrived at by conjugating or inflecting a
verb in voice, mood, tense, number, and person.

The arguments of each verb are noun-phrases
occurring in referential position in input
sentences.

3.2.2 Syntactic Analysis in QUANSY

Syntactic analysis of input sentences is
performed by one major routine PHRSET (Phrase Set),
which calls three subroutines, viz., SUBDETR,
URBDETR, and OBJDETR.

3.2.2.1 SUBDETR

SUBDETR tentatively identifies the subject of a sentence as the continuous string from sentence beginning to predicate beginning. The beginning of a predicate is defined as the first inflected auxiliary or modal verb, or the first verb in the sentence which is not disqualified by being preceded by a quantifier or adjective. A second subroutine is then called, SBSTRUC, which determines the structure of the subject, verifies that the subject is appropriate, checks for pronouns, and determines their antecedents.

3.2.2.2 URBDETR

URBDETR identifies the verb phrase as the maximal string containing inflected verbs, modals, infinitives, adverbs, and other modifiers.

3.2.2.3 OBJDETR

This subroutine is a two-pass process for identifying the object of the verb. The first pass is a preliminary identification of phrases, while the second is a well-formedness check followed by a possible regrouping into new phrases.

3.2.3 Memory Construction

Once an input sentence has been analyzed, it is entered into memory. This procedure is carried out by three routines: MTCHPHR, MTCHRLA, and STUALUE.

3.2.3.1 MTCHPHR

MTCHPHR attempts to match input phrases with existing members of the phrase file. Potential phrase matches are narrowed down by first taking the main noun of the phrase and finding which other phrases it appears in as a noun. For all selected phrases, a right-to-left matching procedure is followed to identify those existing noun-phrases that are identical with the input phrase, including identity of quantifiers and other numerical indicators. A record of near-matches is kept, and other file maintenance is performed.

3.2.3.2   MTCHRLA

MTCHRLA checks for a relation match. The
anchor location (i.e. present active generic form
of the verb) is provided by the term file, and a
search is then performed to find other relational
phrases that have identical inflected verb forms
and modifiers. Attention is next transferred to
the set of arguments of existing relations to
determine whether new input can be merged with
previous information. An example of a merge is:
Input: Bituminous coal reserves are 42% recover-
       able
       The reserves are in Pennsylvania.

Memory: Bituminous coal reserves in Pennsylvania
       are 42% recoverable.

3.2.3.3 STUALUE

STUALUE performs maintenance on all the
pointers of the phrase and term files. In addition, as words occur which have not appeared before (in any form), they are entered into the
file TERMTEM. This file is almost an exact dupli-
cate of the Term file, except that the exact entry
location of any word in the Term file is also
saved. New entry words are coded according to
their usage in the present text. In the dictionary
search, both of these files are accessed, and at
determined intervals they are sorted and merged.

3.2.4 Question Answering

Two additional routines are required to aug-
ment the processes so far described. These are
QUESANA and PHRCMPR, respectively, and together
they provide the most visible aspects of question-
analyzing.

3.2.4.1   QUESANA

QUESANA performs three functions;
(1) translation of questions into their
    corresponding declarative forms;
(2) determination of the nature of the ques-
    tion;
(3) elemination of nuisance questions.

The following question types are dealt with in QUESANA.

1. Imperative

   e.g. "Tell me about bituminous coal reserves in 1975 (please)"

   "Get me information about bituminous coal reserves in 1975 (please)"

2. Declarative

   e.g. "I would like to know about bituminous coal reserves in 1975"

   "I want information about bituminous coal reserves in 1975"

3. Interrogative

   e.g. "What proportion of bituminous coal was shipped by rail in 1973?"

   "Which data source should I consult for trends in petroleum production?"

There are also combination questions:

4. Imperative -Interrogative

   e.g. "Tell me what ERDA has done to support coal gasification research (please)"

5. Declarative - Interrogative

   e.g. "I would like to know what ERDA has done to support coal gasification research"

6. Interrogative - Interrogative

   e.g. "What information is there about what ERDA has done to support coal gasification research?"

There are also nuisance questions:

   e.g. "What do you do?"
   "What techniques do you employ?"
   "What can I look at?"
   "What can I learn from you?"

This list of question types is not exhaustive, although it is indicative of current capabilities.

In determining the nature of the question, QUESANA also determines what probable actions are called for to satisfy the question. For example, some questions are "topical", such as "What is the current unemployment rate?", while others are relational, such as "What is the location quotient of fabricated metal industries in Beaver County?"

QUESANA operates by performing a word-by-word context-sensitive scan of an input question.

3.2.4.2 PHRCMPR

This routine, once called, takes over control of the system (although the system will monitor its operation). It decides when a question is satisfied (or is unable to be satisfied), and when to return control to the system. PHRCMPR performs three basic functions, viz., a relational search, an inferential search, and retrieval.

(1) Relational Searches

For a straightforward request, a very quick response is possible. For more complicated requests, the routine uses the following basic logic in its search;

1. Verify that there is least one relation in memory that would satisfy the question relation;

2. Attempt a match between relevant phrases from the question and phrases of possible relations;

and

3. Find possible phrase substitutes.

The following example of a relational search illustrates this logic. The input question "Are the primary metal industries of Pennsylvania productive?" will be satisfied if the database contains any one of several assertions, including "The primary metal industries of Pennsylvania were productive in 1975." This assertion will also satisfy the question "What did the primary metal industries of Pennsylvania do in 1975?" If the question were more specific, such as "Are the two largest steel companies in Pennsylvania productive?", and the database contained the

assertion "U.S. Steel and Bethlehem Steel are the
two largest steel companies in Pennsylvania", the
system would automatically substitute "U.S. Steel
and Bethlehem Steel" for "the two largest steel
companies in Pennsylvania".

The question-answering system is also capable
of informing a user about the nature of its stored
information, and can invite him to enter additional statements if he so desires. In that case,
PHRCPMPR will ascertain whether the new input is
compatible with existing information before
deciding to accept it.

Should it become obvious that the dialogue is
unprofitable (judged by the user's difficulty in
identifying potential answers), PHRCMPR will
terminate the session and inform the user that it
cannot help him with this particular question.

(2) Inferential Searches

An inferential search, broadly conceived, is
one which proceeds on the basis of properties of
relations. For example, the property of transitivity possessed by the relation "has a higher
index of diversification than" would allow PHRCMPR
to infer the answer "Luzerne County has a higher
index of diversification than Adams County" from
the twin assertions "Luzerne County has a higher
index of diversification than Westmoreland County"
and "Westmoreland County has a higher index of
diversification than Adams County".

Inferential search capabilities of a rudimentary type were developed for PHRCMPR, and are now
being expanded in the research program being
described. A useful subroutine proved to be one
that operated on "How many?" type questions and
the relation expressed by "to have". Thus the
assertions "Pennsylvania has sixty-seven Counties"
and "Each County in Pennsylvania has a county
seat" generate the assertion "Pennsylvania has
sixty-seven county seats".

(3) Retrieval Searches

This capability is very similar to that
developed for the LEADERMART information retrieval
system. Its versatility is most apparent when

interfaced with a numerical data base.

3.3 Answer Determination and Delivery Component

Among other things, QUANSY represents a means for retrieving or otherwise providing factual answers to questions. This is an important step along the way to full knowledge transfer. Another significant step is data retrieval, whether of the numerical or non-numerical kind. The difference between the two is that QUANSY deals primarily with linguistic representations of facts, while data retrieval deals largely with non-linguistic phenomena. Alphanumeric representations of numerical data can, of course, form part of sentences that express facts, but they are not themselves factual assertions.

In order to deal with both kinds of information in constructing knowledge assemblages, we need a means for combining linguistically embodied facts and nonlinguistically represented data. At the level of theory, this means a general formalism in terms of which fact retrieval and data retrieval are subsumed as special cases. Once again, this problem resolves itself into a search for recurrent structural features possessed by both fact retrieval and data retrieval.

The first step in identifying these recurrent structural features is to set up certain categories into which the elementary data items of our knowledge transfer system can be expected to fall. These items will probably be all the presented and analyzed characteristics of several different data collections or bodies of information. Such characteristics will be properties and attributes of data, relationships between data elements, measurements, and so on. For example, a data collection on coal might include such basic compositional characteristics as calorific value, free-swelling index, coke type, microhardness determination, grindability, and mineral matter content. It might also include characteristics pertaining to porosity, surface area, adsorptive capacity, reactivity, permeability, ash fusion, liquefaction, and gasification, together with the economically significant characteristics of yield, ash content, and sulfur content. Each of these characteristics

falls into a particular category, and the types
and numbers of such categories determine different
realms of information.

A piece of information within a certain realm
will have exactly one entry from each of the categories comprising that realm.   For example, a
seam name, seam thickness, sample type, geographical region, equilibrium moisture, dry ash percent-
age, trace element content, specific gravity,
grindability, and a free-swelling index might
constitute one piece of information. Any of its
parts, and any combination of its parts, can be
components of a piece of information. More inter-
estingly, these components cohere with other
components to form new pieces of information which
would not occur explicitly in the data collection.

The combination of different pieces of information into problem-solving knowledge can now be
hypothesized in terms of operations that we perform on categories.   Repeated patterns of categories that occur in problem analyses and solutions will indicate what kinds of information need
to be combined in what ways for solving a problem.
In some cases, the method of combination will be
mathematical, such as a formula for deriving the
properties of coals formed by chemical combinations of several coals. In other cases, the
method of combination might result in aggregated
information. In any event, the various information flows will be concentrated on the basis of
repeated categorical features and issued from a
node in the knowledge transfer network as a
problem-solving knowledge flow. It will be
problem-solving to the extent that it contributes
to a solution on the basis of known solutions to
other similar problems. These pieces of knowledge
can then be entered into the database and re-used
as necessary.

Extraction of knowledge items from the database will require answer-delivery software to
implement the information regeneration and data
synthesizing procedures just described. This software will have several stratified layers corresponding to different stages of answer determination. To begin with, problem recognition software (of the kind exemplified by QUANSY) will be

needed to assist in defining the kind of solution
that is called for by the application in question.
Next, database access software will be required to
perform searching through, say, sets of data
elements. Inquiry response software (again partially exemplified by QUANSY) will be needed to
construct individual pieces of information out of
lower-level categorical items. It is hardly co-
incidental that this construction procedure par-
allels the creation of specially customized reports
from the data elements of records in a database
management system. The parallelism is, in fact,
inevitable in view of our intention to base the
design of a knowledge transfer system on new principles and emerging computer/communications
technology. Finally, a suite of analytical procedures and decision models will be needed to work
in concert with the inquiry response and answer-
delivery software to concentrate and synthesize
information flows into knowledge flows.

3.4 Database Management Component

This component has two related functions.
The first is to massage and direct interactions
between the answer-delivery software that incorporates a decision-maker's logic and the database accesses called for by that logic. The second
function is to control communications and information flows at various interfaces within the
knowledge transfer system. This is more properly
the role of a distributed network manager, i.e. a
number of network processors (usually minicom-
puters) distributed over the knowledge transfer
network. The function is included here for the
sake of completeness.

3.5 Data Sets

The major requirement here will be to organ-
ize heterogeneous bodies of information into data
structures suitable for knowledge transfer. In
our work at Lehigh, we have developed a database
system which permits the use of a single database
structure not only for different bibliographic
bases but also for files of numerical and phenome-
nological data. This ability to handle different
corpora is accompanied by a further capability for
maintaining all of the information pertaining to

a particular record in one location. This enables
us to alter record content without having to
modify several files, as would normally be required in conventional systems. We anticipate
that the demands of knowledge transfer systems
will greatly exceed those of simple retrieval,and
that the ability to deal with a record as a single
entity will become increasingly important.Further-
more, the requirements of knowledge transfer
necessitate a database system in which retrieve/
search tradeoffs can be altered for various system
configurations.

4. The Emergence of Knowledge Transfer Systems

In Section 1, I promised to examine the different responses to the challenge of applying new
computer/communications technology to societal
problems. My examination will be brief, and
couched in terms of two fairly predictable approaches. These are the private sector and public
sector approaches, respectively.

The private sector approach is to regard
information (and derivatively knowledge) as a
commodity, and to identify a marketplace for
information with the customary distinctions between producers, distributors, retailers, and
users. A recent publication observes that

> "More and more companies, agencies
> and activities dealing with information
> as their basic commodity-publishers,
> micro-publishers, systems manufacturers,
> secondary publishers, bibliographic and
> indexing services,information facility
> management services, and many more -
> are finding their place in the information
> marketplace."(4)

A logical next step would be to establish the
handling of information as a discipline separate
from information science. Such is indeed the
case. The same publication states that

> "Information management, just now at
> the beginning of its evolution, will
> become a management discipline in the
> tradition of other management disciplines
> such as finance and marketing."(5)

The public sector response takes the form of planning for a knowledge society. Such a plan would involve the coordination of all information transfer mechanisms to set up a comprehensive, policy-making, scheduling system for targeted goals. Research in this area would focus on the problem of providing strategies for the accumulation, management, and utilization of problem-solving knowledge. The role of a network to facilitate this set of planned activities is much more prominent than it is in the private sector, whose laissez-faire character makes it more difficult to project a widespread commitment to resource-sharing.

An alternative to both of these approaches is to treat information as a semi-public good, that is, a mixture of a purely public good and a purely private good. Dei Rossi (6) develops this notion, and treats price as an allocation mechanism rather than a cost recovery device.

It is not the purpose of this paper to comment on any of these approaches. However, whatever approach is taken, it is clear that the application of problem-solving knowledge to societal problems is by no means a routine extension of today's capabilities. Much remains to be done at a theoretical level to set up the prescriptive rules and principles for achieving socially desirable outcomes, and this paper has attempted to make a start in that direction.

References

1. Information Action, Information Industry Association, 9, 1, (Feb 1977), p.4.

2. L. Chiaraviglio and J. Gehl, "Some Notes on the Planning of Research in the Information Disciplines", Proc. 37th ASIS Ann. Meeting, II, (1974)

3. Ibid., p. 205.

4. Information Action, Information Industry Association, 9, 1, (Feb 1977), p.4.

5. <u>Ibid.</u>, p.5.

6. J.A. Dei Rossi, <u>A Framework for the Economic Evaluation of Pricing and Capacity Decisions for Automated Scientific Information Retrieval Systems</u>, National Bureau of Standards (1973).

The Portent of Signs
and Symbols

Vladimir Slamecka and Charls Pearson

Introduction

In its currently popular trend, information science
shows an almost complete preoccupation with technological
problems and products. A corollary of this preoccupation is
a deep impatience with all efforts which do not immediately
affect information technology. At the same time, the fact
that applied information research has been unable to attain
many of the more important objectives enthusiastically predicted for it twenty years ago is attributed today largely
to the absence in the information field of a core of basic,
or scientific, results--such as were available, for instance,
from physics for aeronautical engineering.

It may behoove us to consider a historical analogy.
Today we credit physics with a major contribution to many of
the triumphs of modern technology, such as the uses of atomic
energy, or space travel and communications. Yet the basic
scientific discoveries which underlie these technological
accomplishments occurred largely during the 16th through the
18th centuries: the language revolution (Copernicus), the
empirical revolution (Galileo), and the theory revolution
(Newton). These efforts built the foundation for physics as
a science, and they provided for its subsequent development
culminating in the engineering accomplishments of our time.

If the reader will tolerate this analogy, then in its
terms the current level of development of the science of
information is somewhere at the level of physics of the 18th
century. We view our own work as belonging to that level of
development: the theory of sign structure proposed here
constitutes, in part, a new language suitable for explicating, empirically, a number of information phenomena, processes, and partial theories. Our research thus aspires to be an

early contribution toward the establishment of a science of information.

The study of information phenomena and processes is not proprietary to any one field of "institutionalized" science. Indeed, such studies have been underway in a number of fields, the more prominent of which are behavioral science, linguistics, communication science, and computer science; and in some instances they have produced partial theories of information. Current research efforts in information phenomena is characterized, however, by a lack of communication between and among the research groups, and by a low utility of the theoretical results obtained. The conclusion one may draw is that these partial theories are insufficiently powerful to provide scientific foundations for the development of more advanced information systems. More general and powerful theories of information phenomena appear to be required for these systems.

We would like to believe that our work, incipient as it is, demonstrates such a portent.

A Theory of Sign Structure

Traditionally, major advances in systematic science have been made by quantification and measurement. In information science, the need for better understanding of the concepts of information measures and measurement is well recognized. Our approach to the study of information measures and measurement is from the viewpoint of semiotics, the study of signs and sign processes. The role that signs play in information processes (that is, in semiotic interactions) is determined by the properties of the sign; in turn, sign properties are determined by the kind of sign and its structure. From this viewpoint, we regard an information measure as any observable property of the sign structure; and the measurement of information as the development of a measurement system for carrying out the observation of that property.

Our purpose in developing a theory of sign structure is to have a tool for explicating the nature of information measurement and its relationship to semiotic processes, and for classifying information measures according to their semiotic dimensionality and interrelationships.

Peirce's Taxonomy of Signs

Throughout our investigations we have had occasion to use several different taxonomies, or classification schemes,

for signs. Of these only the classification by Charles
Peirce (<u>1</u>) has proved to be satisfactory in every empirical
setting for which a classification was wanted. We therefore
ascribe the Peircean scheme an empirical reality, and would
like our theory of sign structure to explain the applicabi-
lity and usefulness of the Peircean scheme in terms of the
structure of the sign.

Peirce defines the sign as a three-place relation:

A sign, or *representamen*, is something which stands
to somebody for something in some respect or capacity
(1, 2.228).

In consequence of every representamen being thus
connected with three things, . . . the science of
semiotics has three branches (1, 2.229).

Peirce called these three branches "pure grammar",
"logic proper", and "pure rhetoric". Subsequently, Charles
Morris called these the three 'dimensions' of semiotics and
gave them their accepted names: syntactics, semantics, and
pragmatics.

Peirce's taxonomy has three classification schemes
(syntactic, semantic, and pragmatic), leading to nine categories of signs.

The syntactic classification defines the 'tone', 'type'
and 'token' sign categories. An example of a tone in linguistics would be a nonterminal node of a phrase structure
diagram, a context category, or a set of allowable (including obligatory) transformations on a sign (word, sentence or
discourse). An example of a tone in logic would be a functional combinator, i.e. a categorical analysis of a sign. An
example of a type in linguistics would be a terminal node of
a phrase structure diagram or a lexical item (word, sentence,
or discourse) at the morphological level, before the phonetic
transformations have been applied. An example of a type of
logic would be a well formed expression (term, formula,
argument). An example of a type in statistical linguistics
would be a general sign of which a particular occurrence
token is a specific instance. Classical linguistics and
classical logic do not concern themselves with the study of
tokens. An example of a token in statistical linguistics
would be the single, particular occurrence of some sign that
actually occurs at a specific point in the computer scan of
a machine readable text. An example of a token in psycho-
linguistics is one actual stimulus that is exposed in a
teescope.

Fig. 1.   The Universal Sign Structure Model

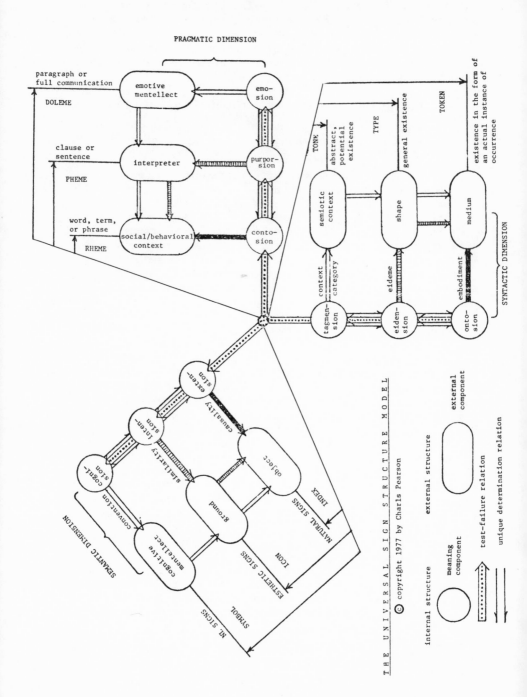

The semantic classification defines the 'index', 'icon' and 'symbol' sign categories. An example of an index in cognitive psychology is Bruner's 'enactive response'. An example from ordinary life would be a pillar of smoke in a dry forest taken by a ranger as a sign for fire, or a knock on a closed door taken by someone on the inside as a sign that someone or something was present on the outside. An example of an icon from cognitive psychology is Bruner's 'ikon'. An example from ordinary life is a paint chip that denotes paint in a can, of the same color as the chip, or a rhythmically repeated note in a melody that holds that music together by the similarities that it establishes. An example of a symbol from cognitive psychology is Bruner's 'symbol'. Natural language signs are all symbolic, including those called 'indexical' and those called 'onomatopoetic'.

The pragmatic classification defines the 'rheme', 'pheme' and 'doleme' sign categories.* An example of a rheme from natural language would be a word or a phrase. An example of a pheme from logic is a statement; from natural language a clause or sentence. An example of a doleme from logic is an argument; from natural language a paragraph or a complete communication.

A Universal Sign Structure Model

The proposed theory of sign structure is embodied in the Universal Sign Structure Model shown in Figure 1. The sign structure model is universal in the sense that it displays the structure of all categories of signs. The theory derived from this model is the outgrowth of the dissertation research of C. Pearson into the structure of symbolic rhemes (2).

The proposed theory consists of three "principles" and nine "representation theorems" which describe the Peircean taxonomy of signs. The Principles are:

The Representation Principle: A sign must consist of a trinary relation, and it must represent. A sign, therefore, consists of three parts: A syntactic structure, a semantic structure, and a pragmatic structure.

The Principle of Internal/External Balance: The internal and the external structure of a sign must be balanced, consisting of exactly one internal component

---

*It must be remembered that Peirce employed a great number of different and differing nomenclatures. The one adopted here was used in (2). Peirce's actual term for doleme was 'deloam' from the Greek δελωμ.

for each external component and vice versa. The internal components are called components of meaning.

<u>The Principle of Additional Structure</u>: Whenever a sign has more than the minimum structure, the additional structure is built up from the center out (as per Figure 1), and for each dimension independently. (For example, from Figure 1 we isolate the minimum structure in Figure 2; if we want to add to it one layer of semantic structure we derive Figure 3, according to the Principle of Additional Structure.

Using the universal sign structure diagram of Figure 1 and these three principles we can now explain the Peircean Taxonomy of signs by means of nine representation theorems. ('Representation' is used here in its mathematical rather than its semiotic sense.) Certain rules of interpretation or translation between the theoretical vocabulary and the observational (or less theoretical) vocabulary will become apparent as we proceed with the proofs of these theorems. The rules of interpretation are obvious, and they form an integral part of the theory. The nine representation theorems are as follows.

<u>Theorem 1</u>: A sign is a tone iff it has exactly one level of syntactic structure. It therefore has one component of syntactic meaning (tagmension) and one external syntactic component (the semiotic context).

<u>Theorem 2</u>: A sign is a type iff it has exactly two levels of syntactic structure. It therefore has two components of syntactic meaning (tagmension and eidension) and two external syntactic components (the semiotic context and the shape of the sign).

<u>Theorem 3</u>: A sign is a token iff it has all three levels of syntactic structure. It therefore has three components of syntactic meaning (tagmension, eidension, and ontosion) and three external syntactic components (the semiotic context, the shape of the sign, and the medium in which it is embodied).

<u>Theorem 4</u>: A sign is an index iff it has exactly one level of semantic structure. It therefore has one component of semantic meaning (extension) and one external semantic component (the object of the sign).

<u>Theorem 5</u>: A sign is an icon iff it has exactly two levels of semantic structure. It therefore has two components of semantic meaning (extension and intension), and two external semantic components (the object of the sign and its

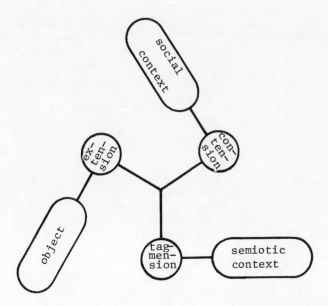

Fig. 2.   The Minimum Semiotic Structure

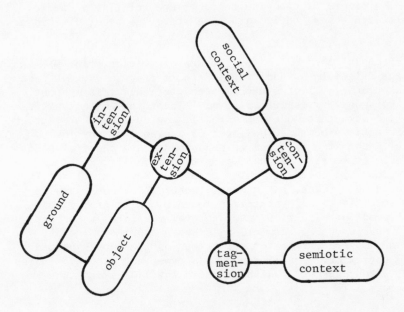

Fig. 3.   A Sign With the Minimum Additional
Semantic Structure

ground).

Theorem 6: A sign is a symbol iff it has all three levels of semantic structure. It therefore has three components of semantic meaning (extension, intension, and cognesion), and three external semantic components (the object, the ground, and the cognitive mentellect of the sign).

Theorem 7: A sign is a rheme iff it has exactly one level of pragmatic structure. It therefore has one component of pragmatic meaning (contension) and one external pragmatic component (the social/behavioral context of the sign).

Theorem 8: A sign is a pheme iff it has exactly two levels of pragmatic structure. It therefore has two components of pragmatic meaning (contension and purposion) and two external pragmatic components (the social/behavioral context of the sign, and its interpreter).

Theorem 9: A sign is a doleme iff it has all three levels of pragmatic structure. It therefore has three internal pragmatic components (contension, purporsion, and emosion), and three external pragmatic components (the social/behavioral context, the interpreter, and the emotive mentellect of the sign).

The proofs of the nine theorems are relatively simple. To illustrate here their nature we state the proof of Theorem 1.

Proof of Theorem 1: By the Representation Principle and the Principle of Additional Structure any sign must have at least one level of syntactic structure and this must be the innermost, or tagmatic, level. According to the Universal Sign Structure Model (Figure 1), the outermost syntactic level consists of the embodiment of a sign in a physical medium. But if a sign had an embodiment in a physical medium it would exist as an actual, single, physically existing individual and could not exist merely as an abstract quality. It would be a token, not a tone; therefore a tone cannot have an ontotic level of syntactic structure. Also from Figure 1, the second (or middle) syntactic level consists of the distinguishable shape, it would exist as a concrete general, serving as an archtype for all tokens of the same type and could not exist, etc. It would be a type, not a tone. Therefore, a tone cannot have an eidontic level of syntactic structure.

Thus a tone has exactly one level of syntactic structure, which is the tagmatic structure. By the Principle of

Internal/External Balance, this structure will consist of
both an internal component and an external component. From
Figure 1 we see that the internal component is tagmension,
the meaning component abstracted from the semiotic context,
and the external component is the semiotic context
itself.   *Q E D*

Interested readers will find all proofs stated in (3).

Investigations Into Sign Structure

This section describes a number of investigations into
the structure of signs and information processes, using the
language and concepts developed and embodied in the theory
outlined above. In selecting these investigations our motivation has been to test and demonstrate the utility of the
language and the theory across as broad a range of basic
information processes as possible; their potential utility
in information technology is broached at the end of this
chapter.

One investigation described (into the nature of definition), concerns all three dimensions of semiotic processes--
syntactic, semantic, and pragmatic. The remaining studies
fall into one each of two categories: syntactic and semantic. So far we have not pursued studies to advance our
understanding of pragmatic structure, although we believe
the Universal Sign Structure Model to be very useful and
promising in this respect.

The Nature of Definition

Definition may be regarded as one of the more important
information processes. We believe that our theory of sign
structure permits us to systematize all previously proposed
concepts of definition.

Many terms associated with definition have appeared in
the literature, but apparently there has been no suggestion
that these may be related to the various components of meaning in any systematic manner. Thus Robinson lists and ana-
lyzes eighteen kinds of definition found in good writers,
(4) without attempting to systematize or interrelate them.
Plato, Pascal, Locke, Whitehead and Russell, and Wittgen-
stein all appear intent on explicating certain concepts of
definition without interrelating them. We do see efforts at
a systematic account of definition in Leibniz and Peirce.
In Leibniz clear and distinct definition leads to clear and
distinct ideas, while Peirce introduces a third mode of
definition that leads to a higher mode of understanding;

these three modes of definition were already understood in
Scholastic ages, however, by such semioticians as Duns
Scotus.

The menetic analysis of definition, first alluded to by
Pearson (2), proceeds from the approach to definition pro-
pounded by J.S. Mill:

> A definition is a proposition declaratory of the
> meaning which it bears in common acceptance, or that
> which the speaker or writer, for the particular pur-
> poses of his discourse, intends to annex to it. (5)

Our theory of sign structure, which identifies meaning
with the internal structure of signs and postulates nine
meaning components, permits us to modify Mill's concept by
introducing the concepts of 'elementary' and 'complete'
definition, as follows:

An ELEMENTARY DEFINITION is one which states one component of the meaning of a term.

A COMPLETE DEFINITION is one which defines all nine components of meaning of a term, and hence incorporates
nine elementary definitions.

The Universal Sign Structure Model predicts nine different kinds of elementary definition. Some of the kinds of
elementary definition and their equivalents identified in
the literature are described in (2).

Syntactic Communication

The Universal Sign Structure Model predicts three levels
of syntactic structure: ontotic, eidontic, and tagmatic.
In the syntactics of natural language these levels may be
identified with phonetics, morphophonemics, and tagmatics,
respectively, although this identification has not been ex-
plicated as yet. Instead, early efforts have concentrated
on using this prediction to explicate the statistical theory
of syntactical communication. The Universal Sign Structure
Model appears to offer the most natural explication for this
theory.

In communication we use actually existing, embodied
signs to carry out actual instances of communication. Communication thus requires the use of sign tokens; this syntactic structure is then our only concern in syntactic
communication theory. Therefore according to our Theorem 3,
the structure of communication is represented by the diagram
in Figure 4.

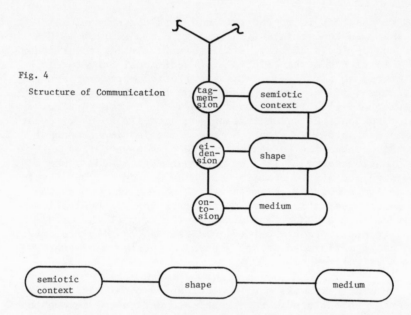

Fig. 4

Structure of Communication

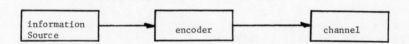

Fig. 5. External Syntactic Structure Rotated

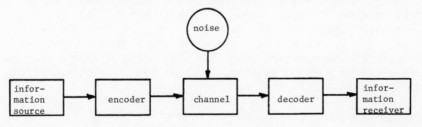

Fig. 6. The Communication Interpretation

Fig. 7. The Communication Model

In the standard theory of syntactic communication as introduced by Shannon (6), however, we are not interested in the meaning of the messages communicated; hence, ignoring the internal portion of the above diagram and rotating the external portion, we obtain Figure 5.

We must now interpret this model in the communication setting. In generating or initiating communication we start with the semiotic context, since this is the first, or innermost, level (from the Principle of Additional Structure). Therefore, we first generate the semiotic context of a sign for communication; next, we add a shape to the sign and its context; and finally, we embody the sign in some physical medium so that the communication can actually be carried out. From these we derive Figure 6; the communication component which generates the context of a sign has been called an 'information source' (7); the component which adds a shape to a sign and its context is called an 'encoder'; the physical medium embodying the sign is called the 'communication channel'. Taking into account the fact that communication includes both a sender and a receiver we derive the traditional communication model (Figure 7). As usually presented, this diagram includes noise, a physical property of every real physical medium.

In most textbooks the "communication model" is usually presented unmotivated. We are able to derive the communication model rationally from the fact that in the theory of syntactic communication we are interested only in the external syntactic structure of tokens. From our viewpoint such theories of communication as presently exist are seen to be theories of communication physics, not general semiotic theories of communication. We suspect that further advances in communication science will require further development of more general semiotic theories.

The semiotic properties associated with tone, type and token phenomena may be used to understand the communication processes associated with each component. We have incorporated this approach into class notes for a senior level course on communication processes (8); it makes these processes quite easy to explain. A textbook on this subject is in preparation (9).

Perception

According to at least one major school of philosophy, the object of perception is signs. Stated more precisely, signs are the vehicle of perception, and the denotata of signs are the objects of perception.

Perception as a semiotic, or information, process is similar to communication, with two important exceptions. First, we are only interested in receiving signs, not in generating or sending them. Second, we are interested in both the internal and the external structure of signs. In order to be received, signs must actually be embodied; hence in perception we are interested in tokens. Furthermore, we are only interested in the syntactic structure. Thus our understanding of the syntactics structure of signs, and particularly our Theorem 3, should be useful for developing psychological theories of perception.

Figure 8 shows a semiotic model of perception, an adaptation of the Universal Sign Structure Model. The major new concept introduced is that of 'menetic valves', which appears useful for integrating many of the isolated findings and theories of particular perceptual phenomena.

From Figure 8 we note that perceptual variables are divided into three categories: ontotic (variables associated with the physical medium), eidontic (variables associated with the semiotic shape of the sign), and tagmatic (variables associated with the tagmatic context). Ontotic variables are equivalent to Stevens' 'psychophysical variables' (10)and Garner's 'energic variables' (11); eidontic variables are synonymous with Garner's 'structural' or informational' variables (11); and tagmatic variables are equivalent to Jenkins' 'contextual variables' (12).

Our threefold catagorization of variables is motivated by the syntactic structure of the sign. It explains such experimental phenomena as Garner's observation that at the informational level of perception all variables fall into two categories (i.e., ontotic and eidontic) having distinct and unique properties; and that there are two kinds of relationship (called by Garner 'state' and 'process') between perceptual variables and the sign processor.

Among the applications of the theory of sign structure to perception investigated at our School of Information and Computer Science are: the neural-quantum model, and the Békésy - Stevens valve (10); the relation between the ontotic and eidontic levels of perception, and the Day - Wood valve (13); the prediction of a "Jenkins valve" for interpreting Jenkins' phenomena (12); and a proposed measurement of the Day - Wood valve.

Syntactic Shape

Our research into the nature of syntactic theory has

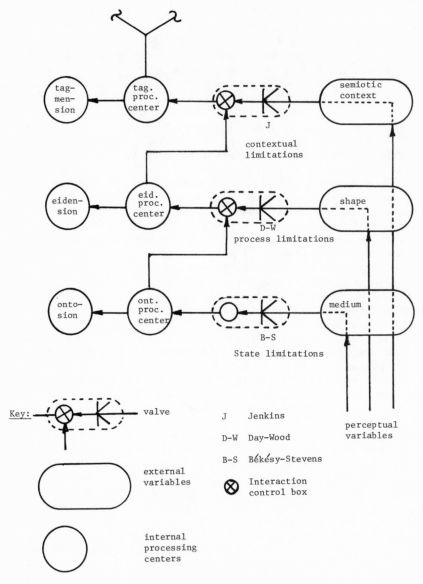

Fig. 8. A Semiotic Model of Perception

concentrated on the eidontic level, with the semiotic concept of shape being of primary interest. This section
reports on our work in this area.

Eidontic Deviance The deviation of the shape of a
natural language sign from the hypothetical norm, or average
shape, of a sign in a given natural language is of considerable interest to information science, for both theoretical
and applied reasons.   To measure such a deviation we have
developed an instrument called the 'eidontic deviometer' or,
in short, 'eidometer' (14). Measurements on artificial word
forms using this instrument are both reliable and precise.

In previous work, Miller, Bruner and Postman showed
that the interpretation of signs is affected by their shape
(15). We expect the eidometer to enable a precise measurement of this phenomena, and hence to lead to a better understanding of the interpretation process. Thus far, we have
redesigned the Miller-Bruner-Postman experiment using an
elementary tachistoscope (teescope) with the stimuluses measured by the eidometer, and have performed successfully an
exploratory trial (the number of interpretation errors as
measured on the teescope is directly and linearly proportional to the eidontic deviance as measured on the eidometer).
This experiment will be refined and carried out with a
sufficient number of subjects to enable satisfactory tole-
rances to be placed on error bounds. This research should
lead to a direct measurement of the redundancy curve for
natural language, a measurement which has not been made before (although Shannon (16) determined upper and lower
bounds for this curve mathematically).

The eidometer permits the redesign of many other classical experiments involving the measurement of word shape, as
well as the design of new experiments investigating various
aspects of semiotic shape. A file of nearly 100 preliminary
experiment designs employing the eidometer has been compiled.

Polygram Frequencies Tables of polygram frequencies are
useful for the generation of artificial word forms and the
study of redundancy in natural language. Since tables for
American English which are publicly available are at least
half a century old and suspect (having most likely come from
counts of military documents), and since access to later and
more general counts which exist requires a security clearance
and "need-to-know", we have prepared a table of polygram
frequencies from a count of 5.5. million letters in the Brown
Corpus of standard American (17).

During the analysis of this count data we discovered a

rank-frequency regularity among the letters. However, un-
like the rank-frequency law of Zipf and Estoup for words,
which is log-log in nature, the regularity for letters is
log-linear in nature. We analyzed all available data for
other alphabets and phonemic systems, and found this relationship to hold in every case. A preliminary literature
search shows no previous mention of this regularity; it is
hoped that after additional analyses (still to be performed)
we may be able to report a discovery of a universal relation
for the shape elements of a system of discrete signs.

   Algorithmic Information In many kinds of signs, shape
is primarily concerned with length and pattern. In 1965
Kolmogorov proposed a measure of shape which is mainly a
measure of the pattern (18); called 'algorithmic information'
or 'complexity', it pertains to the length of the shortest
algorithm that will produce a given sign as its output.

   Patterns, however, can be described verbally, whether
for the purposes of internal coding or of long-term memory
and reproduction. In 1963 Glanzer and Clark, using signs
composed of linear arrays of black and white elements, showed that accuracy of reproduction of patterns was correlated
with the length of description of the patterns (19). In
this case the correlations were based on average rather than
minimum lengths, and length was measured as the number of
words in a natural language (American) description rather
than the number of steps in an algorithm. Using various
outline shapes, Glanzer and Clark further showed that the
length of the description was correlated with judged complexity of the shapes (20); in general, longer descriptions
go with greater difficulty of learning and with greater
judged complexity.

   Conceptually, the Kolmogorov and the Glanzer-Clark
measures are the same. Kolmogorov's measure is a formal or
mathematical model of Glanzer-Clark's empirical measure.

Semantic Structures

   Another area of original investigation which has just
begun concerns the semantic structure of signs. Although
the Universal Sign Structure Model stems from research into
natural language, this same structure should, if it has any
corellation with reality at all, show up also in other disciplines which study sign processes--disciplines such as
philosophy and psychology.

   Analysis A preliminary argument has been developed
which shows the usefulness of the universal structure model

for unraveling philosophical problems. G. E. Moore, an
early twentieth century British philosopher, developed a
paradox which has come to be called Moore's paradox of analysis and may be stated as follows: if the analysis of the
meaning of a word has the same meaning, it is trivial; but if
it has a different meaning, then it is wrong. Moore knew
well that philosophers very often make correct and non-tri-
vial analyses, but he was never able to develop a theory of
analysis which overcame his own paradox. While other philosophers have tried with varying amounts of success, the problem has never been solved completely. The most popular
approach is to say that the problem lies in the formulation
of the paradox, which assumes that meaning is either a single
or wholistic kind of thing which is either completely the
same or else altogether different. Frege (21) and Carnap
(22) assumed that the meaning of signs has two components,
but their assumptions were for entirely different purposes.
Carnap was able to delineate the character of scientific
analysis fairly well with his 'extension' and 'intension',
but he was never able to handle philosophic analysis. Moore
himself said he thought philosophic analysis required something like determining the same objects by the same properties but understanding or cognizing this determination in a
different way.

From our sign structure model (Figure 1), we note that
cognision uniquely determines intension, which in turn
uniquely determines extension; while a difference in extension ensures that two terms will have a difference in intension, which in turn ensures a difference in cognision. We
may therefore state the solution of Moore's paradox as
follows: Scientific analysis requires an identical extension
with a difference in intension, while philosophic analysis
requires an identical intension with a difference in cognision.

Memory Coding Another area we have begun to explore
concerns cognitive representation. Kintsch has reported
three aspects of cognitive memory which he calls 'sensory',
'short term', and 'long term' (23). Bruner has reported
several modes of representation, or coding, including 'enactive', 'ikonic', and 'symbolic' (24). He has studied the
sequence in which these capabilities develop in children and
the rate at which signs can be processed using the various
modes of representation. It would appear as if there were
just one form of coding associated with each aspect of cognitive memory; however, this is not clear because of con-
founding effects on the experiments.

An experimental program is being designed to critically

isolate each memory aspect of the mode of representation that is associated with it. The first experiment, to isolate and determine the characteristics of iconic coding, uses an interference effect suggested by Siegmann (25); in experimental trials the interference effect is well-marked and can be detected easily (26). Additional experiments are planned, including ones using children to verify Bernbach's (27) results.

The advantage of achieving an answer to this question is to allow quantitative measurements of psychology to be used in future investigations of semantic structure. For instance, memory span times, processing rates, and age of development are all quantitative measurements, and all run in the sequence: index, icon, and symbol.

Semantic Linkage Strength   The memory coding experiments described above lead in a natural way to the development of measures for semantic linkage strength.

According to the Universal Sign Structure Model some signs have the semantic field structure shown in Figure 9. One hypothesis that is being investigated (semantic field structure hypothesis) requires all signs to have all six semantic components and all three linkages: the indexical link α; the iconic link β; and the symbolic link γ.

The new concept of α, β, and γ 'linkages' requires empirical establishment. In our thinking, α, β, and γ become empirical measures of semantic linkage strength. They are information measures in the sense of Zunde and Pearson (28) and their practicality must be established by semiotic reinterpretation.

As an example of how one might go about developing measures of linkage strength, consider the iconic linkage strength β. From the paradigm of the Pearson-Seigmann experiment described above we have measures of what may be called iconic interference. From Bernbach's experiment we have motivation for interpreting this as a measure of iconic linkage strength. By generalizing both experiments we may hope to find that the ratio of the short-term memory component to the long-term associative effect varies with the ratio of the iconic interference effect to what may be called 'noninterference'. This may be used both to develop an interval scale for measuring β and for establishing a semiotic reinterpretation for β as an information measure.

Applied Research Potential

We have shown initial evidence of the power of the

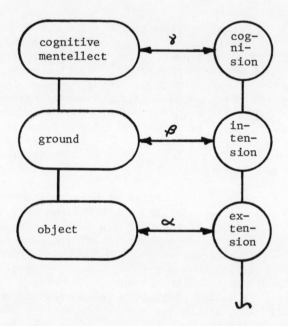

Fig. 9. Semantic Field Structure

proposed theory of sign structure to explicate sign phenomena, the utility of which must be further demonstrated. In
addressing the question of the utility of this research to
practical issues in information processing we may afford to
be mildly speculative. In the body of this report we have
alluded to our current and planned efforts at the applied
plane (e.g., research into aphasia and related brain dis-
orders); we also see our work relevant to a number of applied
problems in information technology. The following illustra-
tions may be given:

o   Now that programming syntactics has reached an initial
     maturity of development, interest in programming theory
     has begun to turn to programming semantics. Early
     studies into programming semantics have concentrated on
     a single-level semantics. Our investigations into the
     structure of signs would suggest, however, that in
     order to achieve the full power of symbolic communica-
     tion of which digital computers and their compilers are
     capable, a three-level semantics is required. A full
     understanding of symbol structure will be required to
     develop such theories.

o   There exist almost no theories of programming pragma-
     tics, and few studies of the subject have ever been
     made. Our studies of sign structure suggest that the
     pragmatic dimension is independent of the semantic
     dimension (a major departure from the Peirce-Morris
     theories), and that it may be at least as important to
     programming theory as the semantic dimension. In order
     to study programming pragmatics and develop appropriate
     theories, an understanding of the pragmatic structure
     of signs is required.

o   Even a cursory look at the notations of control func-
     tions in programming systems shows beyond doubt the
     confusion facing computer programmers and computer
     users. The choice of control functions and their nota-
     tions in individual programming systems has had no
     basis in theoretical principles or in the empiricism of
     human engineering. Our theory of sign structure appears
     to provide a useful framework and a tool for the empiri-
     cal, science-based development of program control func-
     tions and their notations.

o   Many issues in the vast problem area of human inter-
     action with computer-based information systems concern
     the coding of symbols, indexes and icons. Most coding
     studies to-date have dealt with the coding of symbols
     only. Furthermore, there are two types of coding

involved: 1) the creation, change, and interpretation
of the shape of signs; and 2) the storage, linkage, and
retrieval of signs into, in, and from memory. The
coding theories of Shannon and Wiener address the form-
er, while studies by Bruner, Broadbent, Kintch and
others address only the latter. So far, there has been
little reference to the common relationships involved
between these two types of coding and studies have made
either little or naive use of understanding of sign
structure. Since it is plausible to argue that the man/
machine interface problem concerns in part the relationship of two types of coding, it would appear that our
theory is a potential tool for this virgin area of
applied research. This is so because this theory encom-
passes a language and a power to interrelate the semantic and syntactic structure of indexes, icons and
symbols.

Summary

In this paper we have described a new theory of sign
structure which explains the syntactic, semantic, and pragmatic classification of signs due to C. Peirce. The theory
comprises, in part, a language capable of relating studies
of information processes across a range of disciplines, including communication science, psychology, computer science,
and linguistics. The theory and the language have been
applied to explicate empirically such syntactic and semantic
processes as perception, syntactic communication, and memory
coding, and their relevance to selected applied problems of
information engineering has been indicated.

As the common denominator of these efforts is the
study of information processes, the notion of an "information
science" as the umbrella for these studies is appropriate.
Whether or not such a basic science will become institutionalized depends very much on the existence of paradigms relating and unifying its efforts. We view our research firm-
ly as lying in information science, and believe that significant progress along these directions may establish it as
a new paradigm for an alternate group of sciences.

Acknowledgement

This paper is based upon research supported by the
National Science Foundation under Grant No. GN-4092. This
support is sincerely appreciated.

References

1. Peirce, C. S. Collected Papers of Charles Sanders Peirce.* 8 vols. (Ed. by C. Hartshorne and P. Weiss, vols. 1-6; A. Burks, Vols. 7-8). Harvard U. P., 1931-58.

2. Pearson, C. R. Towards an Empirical Foundation of Meaning. Atlanta, Ga., Georgia Institute of Technology, 1977. (Ph.D. thesis)

3. Pearson, C. R.; and Slamecka V. "Semiotic Foundations of Information Science". Final Report (NSF Grant GN-40952), January 1977, School of Information and Computer Science, Georgia Institute of Technology, Atlanta, Ga.

4. Robinson, R. Definition (Corrected Ed., 1965), Oxford, 1954.

5. Mill, J. S. A System of Logic. 1843.

6. Shannon, C. E. "A Mathematical Theory of Communication". Bell Syst. Tech. Jour., 27(1948), p379-423, P623-656.

7. Ash, R. Information Theory. Interscience, 1965.

8. Pearson, C. R. Communication Processes (Course Notes). Atlanta, Ga., Georgia Institute of Technology, School of Information and Computer Science, 1976. (Mimeographed).

9. Pearson, C. R.; and Zunde, P. A Semiotic Approach to the Statistical Theory of Syntactic Communication. (Textbook in preparation.)

10. Stevens, S. S. Psychophysics. Wiley, 1975.

11. Garner, W. R. The Processing of Information and Structure. Wiley, 1974.

12. Jenkins, J. J. "Remember That Old Theory of Memory? Well, Forget It". American Psychologist, 1974, p785-795.

---

*References to the Collected Papers will be given in the standard form where 2.228 refers to vol. 2, paragraph 228.

13. Day, R. S.; and Wood, C. C. "Interactions Between Linguistic and Nonlinguistic Processing". Journal of The Acoustical Society of America., 51(1972), p79.

14. Pearson, C. R.; and Smith, L.; and Ray, J., Jr. "The Eidontic Deviometer: An Instrument for Measuring Shape Deviance in Natural Language". (In preparation).

15. Miller, G. A.; Bruner, J. S.; and Postman, L. "Familiarity of Letter Sequences and Tachistoscopic Identification". Jour. Gen. Psychol., 50(1954), p129-139.

16. Shannon, C. E. "Prediction and Entropy of Printed English". Bell Syst. Tech. Jour., 30(1951), p50-64.

17. Pearson, C. R. "A Table of Polygram Frequencies". (In Preparation.)

18. Kolmogorov, A. N. "Three Approaches to the Quantitative Definition of Information". Problems of Information Transmission. 1(1965), p1-7.

19. Glanzer, M.; and Clark, W. H. "Accuracy of Perceptual Recall: An Analysis of Organization". Journal Verbal Learn. and Verbal Behavior, 1(1963), p289-299.

20. Glanzer, M.; and Clark, W. H. "The Verbal-loop Hypothesis: Conventional Figures". American Journal Psychol. 77(1964), p621-626.

21. Frege, G. "Uber Sinn and Bedeutung". Zeitschr. f. Philos. u. Philos. Kritik, (1892), p100. Reprinted as "On Sense and Reference" in The Philosophical Writings of Gottlob Frege. Tr. by M. Black.

22. Carnap, R. Meaning & Necessity. University of Chicago Press, 1958.

23. Kintsch, W. Learning, Memory and Conceptual Processes. Wiley, 1970.

24. Bruner, J. S. "On Cognitive Growth, I & II". In Bruner-1, p1-67, 1966.

25. Siegmann, P. J., personal communication, 1975.

26. Pearson, C. R.; Siegmann, P. J.; and Shin, K. J. "An Experimental Investigation of Iconic Coding". (In preparation.)

27. Bernbach, H. A. "The Effect of Labels On Short-Term
    Memory for Colors With Nursery School Children".
    Psychon. Science, 7(1967), p149-150.

28. Zunde, P.; and Pearson C. R.   Information Measurement
    (Textbook in preparation.)